How We Got Our Denominations

*What is the church? The church is man when his awed soul goes
    out,
In reverence to a mystery that swathes him all about.
When any living man in awe gropes godward in his search;
Then in that hour, that living man becomes the living church,
Then, though in the wilderness or in waste, his soul is swept along
Down naves of prayer, through aisles of praise, up altar stairs of
    song.
And where man fronts the Mystery with spirit bowed in prayer,
There is the universal church—the church of God is there.*

—SAM WALTER FOSS

HOW WE GOT
OUR DENOMINATIONS

A PRIMER ON CHURCH HISTORY

by

STANLEY I. STUBER

Author of
The Living Water
The Story of Clifton Springs
etc.

ASSOCIATION PRESS : NEW YORK : 1948

Acknowledgment is made to Charles Scribner's Sons, Lothrop, Lee & Shepard Co., The Macmillan Company, G. P. Putnam's Sons, The Houghton Mifflin Co., University of Chicago Press, Funk and Wagnalls Co., D. Appleton-Century Co., The Pilgrim Press, Doubleday and Doran Co., and Blue Ribbon Books, for permission to quote from their copyrighted works.

DEDICATED
TO THOSE
WHO KEEP ME YOUNG
IN MIND AND IN SPIRIT

My Wife
HELEN
Bates College, '25

My Children
ROSCOE
Denison University, '49

SYLVIA   LOIS
Bates College, '50   RHS, '50

CONTENTS

Part III
THE PROTESTANT REFORMATION

Part IV
THE MODERN CHURCH

PREFACE

This primer on church history is written primarily for the Christian layman. It has been designed, not only for general reading, but for study courses in summer assemblies, schools, and colleges, and in the senior high and adult departments of church schools. At the end of each chapter are discussion topics and lesson assignments which take church history out of the pages of a book and place it in the very center of contemporary life.

Today there is no more lively topic of discussion than denominationalism and whether or not we should have church union. Most Protestants are agreed that there should be a much closer cooperation among the denominations; many go so far as to advocate some form of federation. A few champion total union.

There is almost general rejoicing when two or more denominations unite to form a single body. But when it comes to church union itself or the formation of one great Protestant organization, the agreement disintegrates, and the discussion increases in volume and intensity.

The author does not look upon the various denominations as creations of the devil. They are instruments which have been formed to serve God. As this study will reveal, all of them were created for some good purpose—or at least the purpose was judged "good" at the time. Many of them were natural developments growing out of the spirit of the Reformation. Some of them grew up with America. Others of them came about through issues involved in the Civil War. While, in the latter case, history has healed a few of the divisions, in other respects new divisions have since been created, chiefly around theological differences. Laymen often get very impatient with these man-made separations which seem to be stimulated and cultivated by "narrow-

minded" clergymen.[1] These Christian laymen, including young
people, are increasingly demanding cooperation and union
wherever possible. They deem it a waste of time, money, and
energy, and a diversion of the Christian spirit, to have over-
lapping and competing denominations.

Protestantism certainly needs to be strengthened. It has a
great work to do in the areas of social justice, religious liberty,
Christian education, world missions, and evangelism. It has a
pagan world to confront and to win for Christ. In this struggle,
it needs the full, united support of all the various denominations.
Instead of fighting one another, as so often is the case, they must
from now on unite to form a united front against a united
enemy. They must consider anew the contribution they have to
make to a needy world, heading in the direction of moral,
spiritual, and physical ruin. The Christian thing for them to do
would be to throw their resources into a united world program.
In this way, working as a team, they can accomplish together
what it would never be possible for them to achieve separately.

I, for one, do not want a super-church with an authoritarian
ecclesiastical hierarchy. Such a system of church union might
well cause more problems than it would solve. What I would
like is a unified, coordinated Protestant program extending over
a period of twenty-five years or more, in which each denomination would have a real part and make a distinct contribution.
This might well be Protestantism's *first* Twenty-five Year Plan!
Through press, radio, and motion pictures, through preaching
and teaching, through Christian practice and action, Protestantism could then conduct a world-wide mission program which
might be strong enough to turn the tide against the present
forces of evil.

Denominations working alone will never be strong enough
to save the world. Working together they would not only have
the strength of their own respective denominations, but the
multiplied spiritual and moral power of a united, creative

---

[1] Of the two hundred and fifty-six denominations in the United States
two hundred of them represent a membership of only about 2 per cent of
the total.

Christian force. Now that most denominations have completed their own relief and rehabilitation campaigns, the next step is to bring together their newly created services and missionary endeavors into one great world-wide Crusade for Christ. If this is not done, of what real value will be all our multiple million-dollar promotional campaigns? Will they not, if left alone, magnify their differences and develop separate competing programs?

My hope is that readers of this book will join me in the prayer that through the proposed National Council of Churches, which will unite all of the interdenominational councils here in the United States, and through the World Council of Churches—or, if necessary, by some other means—a World Christian Mission may be established which will be so vital, creative, and challenging as to bring into sharp focus the mighty elements of strength represented in our denominations.

STANLEY IRVING STUBER

New York City
May, 1948

· 1 ·

FROM JESUS TO THE CHURCH

THE KINGDOM PRECEDES THE CHURCH

Jesus knew nothing about the "Christian Church." His mission was to establish the kingdom of God in the hearts of men. He thought little about organization and a great deal about life. In fact he only referred to the word "church" twice, and there is a question whether or not he meant an organization when he used the term.

It is interesting to note the growth in the usage of the word "church," as found in the New Testament. It is used only two times in the Gospels, which reflect Christ's own teachings, but over a hundred times in the other books. On the other hand, the word "kingdom" occurs over a hundred times in the Gospels but not over twenty-five times in the remaining books.

As time passed, the word "church" came to be used in place of the word "kingdom" by the Christian writers, although it did not have such a broad and deep meaning as Jesus' kingdom of God.

See Act 8:12 – Act 20:25
Act 28:24 28:31

THE CUSTODIAN OF FAITH

The Church was essentially the result of the need of fellowship among the early Christians. The kingdom had to have a home somewhere, so it built for itself the organization which we today call the Church of Christ. It was to be used to promote the interests of the kingdom, being a custodian of the faith. It was to be used only as a means to an end—the end being the kingdom of God. Just how far Jesus intended for his kingdom to become organized is a question. It is certain that he would

13

not trust even the best organized church, as such, unless it had the spirit of the kingdom burning within it.

It should be clearly understood that Christianity is not the organization called the Church, but is rather the spirit and program back of the organization which Jesus called the kingdom. If the Church is to fulfill its purpose, it must have these five functions, given by William Adams Brown. He says that every church worthy of the name has at least five main functions which it discharges in the life of its worshipers:

1. It is the organ of their common worship.

2. It is the school in which they are instructed in the meaning of their religion.

3. It is the instrument of their moral discipline.

4. It is the agency through which they combine for common worship.

5. It is the means through which the tenets of their religion are propagated.

THE DANGER OF OVEREMPHASIS

Jesus always stood for simplicity and sincerity in religion. He was relatively indifferent to the forms and institutions of his own day, and at times definitely violated them. Why? Because his kingdom was of the spirit, and not of the letter.

Organization is a good means, but should never be confused with high ideals and noble purposes, as often is the case. To make matters worse, it is always leaving its place as a means and becoming an end in itself. In this way people come to keep the form for its own sake, rather than using it as a helpful means. As Francis Greenwood Peabody says in *The Church of the Spirit*:

The soul of the church may languish while its body still thrives, and the end for which the church exists may be forgotten in the devotion to the means.

The Pharisees put the emphasis in the wrong place—upon form and show. Jesus said that they were wrong. The Church of the Middle Ages did likewise, and Martin Luther said that it was greatly mistaken. The Church of today is doing the same thing, and fearless men are trying to point out the wrong. Their cry is: "Back to the principles of Christ!"

THE TEST OF REAL CHRISTIANITY

"By their fruits ye shall know them," said the Master. This can be applied to all sects, doctrines, and religious movements, as well as to life. The great question is: "Do they promote the kingdom?" If they help to make life sweeter and more worth while, if they kindle a zeal in the hearts of men for the Great Teacher, if they help to make the world a brotherhood, then they are instruments of the kingdom. If not, then they should be sacrificed for the good of all concerned, and some other means should be tried.

> Though Love repine, and Reason chafe,
>   There came a voice without reply,—
> 'Tis man's perdition to be safe,
>   When for the truth he ought to die.
>   RALPH WALDO EMERSON

QUALIFICATIONS FOR MEMBERSHIP

Jesus' qualifications for membership in his kingdom were very simple, and are summed up best in the word "conversion," which means turning about or around. This change involves both repentance and faith—faith being emphasized the most, because of its positive nature. To join the kingdom one must:

1. Repent of past sins (Mark 1: 14).
2. Believe in the kingdom message (Matthew 7: 24).
3. Do the will of the Father (Matthew 7: 24).

"Follow me and I will make you fishers of men," said the Master to his disciples. These are very challenging words, showing that he saw a plenteous harvest in the future and a great need for reapers. He wanted real workers, and so he chose twelve humble men and trained them in fishing for men. How? —by being their companion and example; by fishing with them;

by setting before them the principles of the kingdom and a missionary ideal which is only now being realized.

Why did these practical men accept these ideals and follow this man from Galilee? The answer is easy: the Man! They accepted *him* long before they did his teachings. He was irresistible! He has been so all through the ages. Here, then, is the secret of the power of the Kingdom-Church: Jesus, the giver of a more abundant life. He is the keystone of Christianity. He is the hope of the Church.

> If Jesus Christ is a man,—
>   And only a man,—I say
> That of all mankind I cleave to him,
>   And to him will I cleave alway.
>
> If Jesus Christ is a god,—
>   And the only God,—I swear
> I will follow Him through heaven and hell,
>   The earth, the sea, and the air.
>   RICHARD WATSON GILDER

HELPS FOR STUDY

Written Work

1. What relationship has the kingdom to the Church?
2. What has been the real purpose of the Church throughout the ages? What are its functions?
3. What is the danger in religious institutions?
4. How can the Church be tested?
5. Give the qualifications for membership in the kingdom.

Oral Discussion

1. What attitude did the Roman Government take toward Christianity?
2. Does the organization of the Church, as it is today, help or hinder the realization of the kingdom?
3. How do the requirements for membership in your church compare with Jesus' standards?
4. Why do we make so much of creeds and doctrines, while ignoring the basic teachings of Jesus?

Special Assignments

1. Give an outline of each of the parables of Jesus which deal with the growth of the kingdom.

2. Comment on this statement by Glover: "With all his wide outlook on mankind, his great purpose to capture all men, Jesus is remarkable for his omission to devise machinery or organization for the accomplishment of his ends."

3. Read the Sermon on the Mount.

4. Write a book report on some life of Jesus.

5. Visit a church of a denomination outside your own fellowship.

·2·

ONE GREAT FAMILY

THE BIRTHDAY OF THE CHURCH

When was the birthday of the Church? It is impossible to say just when, for the Church was in existence before the day of Pentecost. But because so many consider it the day the Christian Church was first realized, and since it was a red-letter day in its history, the day of Pentecost is usually regarded as the birthday of the Church. (Of course, the disciples were not called Christians at this time.)

It was the seventh Sunday after the resurrection of Jesus; the disciples were waiting for the coming of the Holy Spirit which Jesus had promised them. The upper chamber, probably where the Last Supper was eaten, served as their meeting place. Here, grouped together with a common purpose, this little band of believers had begun to develop a strong bond of unity. Once they had been disciples of the Master; now they were brothers in Christ.

During this meeting, the Holy Spirit came. It came with power, interrupting their devotions and sounding like a great wind. Finally, it rested upon each of the heads of the disciples like tongues of fire. It was then that they became conscious of an inward transformation which gave them marvelous spiritual illumination. Being thrilled with the new joy and confidence, they began to praise God for their glorified Lord with such zeal that those who heard them from the outside thought surely that they were drunk. In amazement, these people, who were mostly foreigners visiting Jerusalem, thought that they heard the disciples glorifying God in utterances that were to each

18

hearer like his own. Some of them were impressed, but others ridiculed it as the result of a feast.

Following this great initial impulse, three thousand men, in addition to many women, were added in a single day. After this, the membership rapidly increased, until it became five thousand (Acts 4: 4). A little later, "a great company of the priests were obedient to the faith" (Acts 6: 7). And so the family grew, being led by the spirit of the Master. The rapid growth of the Church may be accounted for in the following manner:

1. The new teaching did not involve any break with the old Jewish faith or life.
2. Jesus was expected to return in the near future.
3. The period was full of evangelistic activity.
4. Life was made adventurous for its members.

Here is opened before us the Christian Age. At this time the followers of Christ received a new sense of their oneness with God and with one another. It was the day when the evangelistic activity of the Christian Church began and when the disciples first realized that their mission was to be witness bearers of the living Lord throughout the then known world.

JESUS ACCEPTED AS THE MESSIAH

The followers of the Master were now ready to go a step farther than the Jewish Church ever dared to go. They accepted Jesus as the Messiah. Here lies the secret of the enthusiasm of primitive Christianity. No matter what we may personally believe concerning the physical resurrection of Jesus, we must admit that it was the belief that Jesus rose from the grave which colored the whole life of this period and gave the disciples the triumphant power of the message which they proclaimed. By accepting Jesus as the Messiah, the Christian Church received a more abundant life.

LAW, THE DRAWBACK

Jesus never abolished the religious law of his day, so the Jewish Christians regarded Christianity merely as a continuation of their own religion. As Glover explains:

They accepted Jesus as the Messiah and believed that the Jews were to be saved by the law plus Jesus, while Gentiles were to be saved by Jesus plus the law.

This made Christianity hardly more than a spiritualized Judaism. Even Peter, up until the later part of his life, taught exactly this. Paul's teaching of justification by faith was actually defeated in the early days of the Church.

The persecution, however, caused a split in the Christian ranks. Those believers who remained at Jerusalem were mostly Hebrews who clung to the legalistic forms, while those who went away were unable to continue all the Jewish forms, and so came to put less and less emphasis on them. This caused hard feelings, for the Church at Jerusalem had no sympathy for these people who had been influenced by the Greco-Roman world. Here began the controversy between the "Fundamentalists" and "Modernists," which has continued ever since, much to the discredit of the Christian cause.

Two Fearless Men

Peter was unquestionably the leading light of the early Church. His impulsive nature and natural ability of leadership fitted him to take command. He was bold and confident; and, being controlled by a new regulative power which he found in Christ, his words became marvelously effective against the consciences of his hostile hearers. This was a time for action; the enemy pressed hard on every side. Peter, the fearless, gave his very best to the cause of Christ, even his life. Some of the outstanding events in his life are to be found in the following passages: Acts 1: 15, 2: 14-36, 3: 1-8, 5: 1-11, 5: 18, 9: 32-35, 9: 36-42, 10: 1-33, 12: 1-19, and 15: 7-11.

We first hear of Stephen when he was chosen as one of the seven intrusted with the apportionment of the common fund. He soon won fame beyond the routine of his office as a keen and resistless champion of the cause. With his liberal Hellenistic training, he had a much larger view of the mission and genius of Christianity than did most of the Jews. Because of this, he was hated by the conservative Jews, who cast their bigotry on him. They seized him and brought him before the Sanhedrin, charging him with blasphemous utterances against the temple. Stephen's words were distorted by false witnesses. He began a speech in defense, but he never finished it. Before he had half finished, members of the Sanhedrin grew wild with rage and rushed upon him. They dragged him outside the city, where they stoned him to death. Thus Stephen died, "his face as it had been the face of an angel," and with the words, "Lord, lay not this sin to their charge," upon his lips. Here the Church received its first baptism of blood and its first martyr.

> I cannot hide that some have striven,
> Achieving calm, to whom was given
> The joy that mixes man with heaven:
>
>   .   .   .   .
>
> Which did accomplish their desire,
> Bore and forebore, and did not tire;
> Like Stephen, an unquenched fire.
>
> He heeded not reviling tones,
> Nor sold his heart to idle moans,
> Tho' cursed and scorn'd, and bruised with stones:
>
> But looking upward, full of grace,
> He prayed, and from a happy place
> God's glory smote him on the face.

ALFRED TENNYSON

GROWTH THROUGH PERSECUTION

The murder of Stephen was the beginning of a period of persecution against the Christians. They were dragged to prison, and their meeting places were destroyed. The only practical thing these assailed Christians could do was to take refuge in flight or in hiding. But since hardship or persecution often tends to make for strength, the Church received much good from this struggle. It helped:

1. To purge out the false or half-hearted members.

2. To end the unrealistic practice of sharing all things in common.

3. To spread far and wide the Christian teaching.

4. To develop leaders who were earnest in the spirit and instructed in the faith.

5. To cause a growth in the knowledge of Christian living, organization, and church worship.

> The pure, the bright, the beautiful,
>   That stirred our hearts in youth,
> The impulses to wordless prayer,
>   The dreams of love and truth;
> The longing after something lost,
>   The spirit's yearning cry,
> The strivings after better hopes—
>   These things can never die.
>
> CHARLES DICKENS

HELPS FOR STUDY

Written Work

1. What happened at Pentecost?

2. What was the dividing point between the Christian and the Jewish Church?

3. In what way was the law a drawback to the Church?

4. Who were Peter and Stephen?

5. Give five results of the persecutions.

Oral Discussion

1. What really took place in the Upper Room on the day of Pentecost?

2. What attitude should be taken in regard to the miracles?

3. How should this statement be interpreted: "I say unto you that thou art Peter, and upon this rock I will build my church; and the gates of hell shall not prevail against it." (Matthew 16: 18)?

4. What keeps us from having church unity?

Special Assignments

1. Read the first twelve chapters of Acts.
2. Make an outline of Peter's speech given on the day of Pentecost.
3. Make a list of the characteristics that develop heroes.
4. Write a short paper on "The Psychology of Conversion."

·3·

THE CHURCH AT ANTIOCH

And the disciples were called Christians first at Antioch.

THE CITY OF THE FIRST GENTILE CHURCH

Barnabas goes to the church at Antioch (Acts 11: 22, 23).
Paul is chosen as the partner of Barnabas (Acts 11: 25, 26).
Relief is sent to the brethren in Judea (Acts 11: 29).
The church at Antioch sends forth two missionaries (Acts 11, 12).

Antioch was the capital of Syria. It was next to Rome and Alexandria in importance, being situated a few miles from the mouth of the Orontes River and having a population of half a million. Its streets and buildings are said to have been among the finest in the world. In many ways, it was a center of learning. Its fame, however, was due to its wealth and lax ways of living. The city was corrupt. Many Jews lived here, but the larger part of the population were proselytes. This pagan city was destined to become the key city for the expansion of early Christianity.

Jerusalem, Antioch, Rome—these three cities are the stepping stones along which Christianity went forward from its Jewish cradle to Gentile missions and thence to world dominion.—WILLIAM HILL

Christianity spread in its early days chiefly by the word of mouth of its disciples.[1] Here was a time when hearts were so overpowered with the good news that it was impossible for them to remain silent. They had been filled with the spirit of goodness and desired others to share in the same experience.

---

[1] See Kenneth Latourette's *History of the Expansion of Christianity.*

24

Among the disciples at Antioch were to be found certain men who were regarded as leaders because of their great zeal in Christ. These men were Barnabas, Simeon Niger, Lucius of Cyrene, Manaen, and Paul. A little later we find this church appointing two of these leaders, Barnabas and Paul, to go forth and preach the gospel to the Gentiles.

It is impossible to say too much about the influence Paul had on early Christianity. Although there were other missionaries before Paul, such as Philip in Samaria and Peter in Cæsarea, he holds first claim to the name of Apostle to the Gentiles. It was Paul, and Paul alone, who first saw what freedom in Christ meant. He first introduced Christ to the whole world. But that was not all. He also built many homes for Christ on foreign soil. It was not his intention to build up a new religion, for that had already been done by Jesus. Paul's whole strength is to be found in the fact that he preached Christ, the risen Savior.

FOLLOWING PAUL AND BARNABAS ACROSS THE EMPIRE

They say good-by at Seleucia.

A visit is made at Barnabas' home at Salamis.

They call on a Roman proconsul at Paphos.

John Mark gets tired at Perga and returns home.

"Almost the whole city" comes out to hear Paul preach at Antioch of Pisidia.

They are mistaken for gods at Iconium.

Paul stands a man on his feet at Lystra and in return they stone him until he was thought to have been dead.

Many disciples are made at Derbe.

They retrace their steps through Lystra, Iconium, and Antioch of Pisidia.

They set sail from Attalia to Antioch in Syria.

The results of this first missionary journey were far-reaching. At Lystra a youth named Timothy, who later became one of the greatest leaders in the early Church, heard the call to service. At Derbe a devoted disciple of Jesus was made, called Gaius. And at Iconium, the city from which the two missionaries had to flee for their lives, there arose in time an influential center of Christian work. Who knows what our feeble efforts may lead to? We all should take courage from the lives of these heroic pioneers, who "suffered the loss of all things, if only they might gain Christ." Time will give its rewards and revelations. Henry van Dyke expresses this thought in "A Lost Word of Jesus":

> Hear the Master's risen word!
> > Delving spades have set it free,—
> > Wake! the world has need of thee,—
> Rise, and let thy voice be heard,
> Like a fountain disinterred.
> > Upward-springing, singing, sparkling;
> > Through the doubtful shadows darkling:
> Till the clouds of pain and rage
> Brooding, o'er the toiling age,
> > As with rifts of light are stirred
> > By the music of the word;
> Gospel for the heavy-laden, answer to the labour's cry;
> "Raise the stone and thou shalt find me; cleave the
> > wood, and there am I."

ORGANIZATION OF THE CHURCH AT ANTIOCH

The organization of the church at Antioch was like that of most of the early churches of this period, although allowance should be made for minor variations. Therefore, with this understanding, this church will be used as a sample for all the rest. In the first place, the basis of the organization was fraternal equality. It was fundamentally democratic in principle and, so far as it could be, in practice. All Christians of the city constituted the church—as at Jerusalem, Ephesus, and Corinth. It is supposed that they had more than one place of meeting, since the church often had thousands of members. The church at Jerusalem was the Mother Church and the seat of authority, although each church was free in itself.

The church had two classes of officers: elders (sometimes called bishops, ministers, or pastors) and deacons. These officers attended to all the affairs of the church, but only under the direction of the congregation. They had no priestly power and were answerable to the congregation, which appointed them for all their actions. Apostles, prophets, and evangelists, on the other hand, exercised their duties by divine appointment and were not answerable to the churches.

The worship was very simple. There was singing and prayer, followed by a reading from the Old Testament with an exhortation on the passage. There was no formal sermon. The service was much like the modern prayer meeting of a generation ago, with a great deal more enthusiasm injected into it. Sometimes special features were added, such as reminiscences of what Jesus had done and said, told by someone who had heard him or by those who had been with his disciples. The services usually took place at night. The Lord's Supper was celebrated with bread and wine, as the memorial of the Lord's death. Often a meal was connected with this service. There is good evidence that baptism was administered to believers only, by immersion in water, in the name of Jesus.

James Hastings Nichols points up the practices of this "communion of saints" when he says, in his *Primer for Protestants:*[2]

This consciousness of the community of all Christians everywhere was nourished especially by two dramatic ceremonies Jesus had commended to his disciples as symbols of the life of the kingdom before there was any thought of a "church." Many of Jesus' disciples probably came to him from John the Baptist. In any case the followers of Jesus adopted John's practice of a ceremonial bath as a sign of the washing away of sins in repentance. In addition to this rite of initiation into the new "body," the disciples preserved at their regular meal together the dramatized parable Jesus had presented to the twelve on the night in which he was betrayed. In the joy of the vindication of the resurrection they remembered the obedience unto death which had sealed the new covenant and rejoiced in the experience of Christ's continued fellowship. To this very day in the evangelical Lord's Supper the experience of the disciples at

---

[2] James Hastings Nichols, *Primer for Protestants* (New York, Association Press, 1947), pages 21-22.

Emmaus is repeated again and again. Men have departed from the table-fellowship of Christians with a sudden recognition that the living Christ had been present among them, and have said to each other in wondering joy, "Did not our hearts glow within us?"

HELPS FOR STUDY

Written Work

1. What was the character of the city of Antioch?
2. Who were some of the leaders of the church, and how did they happen to be chosen?
3. Give the places of Paul's first missionary journey.
4. What was the organization of the church at Antioch?

Oral Discussion

1. Why did Paul and Barnabas make good partners in missionary work? Discuss the character of each.
2. How did the church at Antioch differ from the one at Jerusalem?
3. Was Paul the founder of Christianity, as we know it today?
4. What was his influence on Christianity?
5. Which is the more important for a person to have, the religion *about* Jesus or the religion *of* Jesus?

Special Assignments

1. Outline Paul's second and third missionary journeys, noting the outstanding events.
2. Make a list of the different terms which Paul gave to Christian doctrine.
3. Write a paper on the contribution which Paul made to Christianity.
4. Read a life of Paul.

· 4 ·

UNDER FIRE
. . . the Church under Persecution

They love all men, and are persecuted by all.

ANONYMOUS

THE PERIOD OF PERSECUTION

During the first half of the apostolic age, the Christians enjoyed a short period of peace, except for a few cases of ill-treatment by the Jews. The Roman Government used them justly, though perhaps somewhat contemptuously. Later the Romans took up the persecution, and strange as it may seem rulers like Trajan and Marcus Aurelius were among the worst persecutors, while some of the most infamous emperors were indifferent and sometimes even favorable to Christianity. The persecution of the early days was only spasmodic and limited, having no backing from the Roman Government, while the persecutions of a later date were more general and conducted under the command of the emperor himself. The severity of the persecution depended upon the whims and feelings of each individual emperor.

The outline of the persecution, from Nero to Constantine, is as follows:

First Period

64 A.D.	Nero	First persecution of Christians by Romans.
69– 79	Vespasian	No definite persecution.
79– 81	Titus	Policy of Nero continued.

29

81– 96   Domitian . . . . Severity increased, both in Rome and in the provinces.
96– 98   Nerva . . . . Tolerance of the Christians.
98–117   Trajan . . . . No wanton persecution, but the laws and religion of the empire rigidly upheld.
117–138   Hadrian . . . . Christianity judged rather trivially.
138–161   Antonius Pius . . . . Christians protected.
161–180   Marcus Aurelius . . . . . Persecution encouraged.

Second Period

180–193   Commodus . . . . Friendly to the Christians.
193–211   Septimius Severus . . . Christians persecuted with severity.
211–217   Caracalla . . . . Christianity tolerated.
218–222   Heliogabalus . . . . Christianity tolerated.
222–235   Alexander Severus . . . Christianity given a place in his cosmopolitan faith.
235–238   Maximinus . . . . Christians put to death.
244–248   Philip the Arabian . . . Christians not punished.

Third Period

249–251   Decius . . . . Universal persecution.
253–260   Valerian . . . . Persecution increased.
260–268   Gallienus . . . . Further persecution forbidden.
270–275   Aurelian . . . . Old laws enforced with renewed vigor.
284–305   Diocletian . . . . Harshest persecution.
    311   Galerius . . . . Limited toleration.
    313   Constantine . . . . Christianity made a state religion.

WHY THE CHRISTIANS WERE PERSECUTED

"Does not the Emperor punish you justly?" Celsus asked the Christians. "Should all do like you, he would be left alone— there would be none to defend him." This was the common belief held among the Romans. They began to fear this secret body of irresistible people who were called Christians. And why should they not have cause to fear? Christianity caused trouble wherever it went! It was opposed to the whole governmental, social, and religious systems of Rome. It broke up homes, setting the husband against the wife, the children against their parents, the slave against his master. It caused the traders and priests of the temple a loss of profits, for these Christians worshiped with neither image nor shrine. It would have nothing to do with the licentious and cruel amusements of the Romans. It refused the duty of a loyal citizen and would hold no office. It objected to all military service and refused to worship the emperor. As its meetings were held at night, with both sexes present, they were mistaken for carnivals of lust, where, as the Romans thought, their offspring of passion were sacrificed to their one god. Also, it was intolerant of all other religions. All this tended to make the Romans look upon Christians as the worst of degenerates, who should be cast from society. No punishment could be too severe for these people called Christians.

Besides all this, they were also blamed for every fire, war, pestilence, flood, famine, earthquake, and other disaster. This, the Romans thought, was merely the vengeance of the gods upon these disbelievers, "who denied the many gods and worshipped but one, and who discarded all images—even that of the Emperor." Nothing good could ever come from these Christians. Really, it took courage to be a Christian in those days!

NERO AMUSES HIMSELF

In July, 64 A.D., a terrible fire, lasting for several days, destroyed most of Rome. The citizens at once suspected Nero of the crime. He had fiddled while the city burned, in order that he

. . . might revel in the wild scenes of its flames and the misery of the flying citizens, or glorify himself by building a new city upon the ashes of the old.

Nero, however, was not ready to shoulder any of the blame. He at once cast it upon the Christians; and since they were hated for the peculiar lives which they were supposed to have led, the charge was easily fixed upon them. The persecution which followed was of a very savage nature. Tacitus, a writer of that time, describes it in a very vivid manner:

Therefore, at the beginning, some were seized who made confessions; then, on their information, a vast multitude were convicted, not so much of arson as of hatred of the human race. And they were not only put to death, but subjected to insults, in that they were either dressed up in skins of wild beasts and perished by the cruel mangling of dogs, or else put on crosses to be set on fire, and, as day declined, to be burned, being used as lights by night. Nero had thrown open his gardens for the spectacle, and gave a circus play, mingling with the people, dressed in a charioteer's costume or driving in a chariot. From this arose, however, toward men who were, indeed, criminals and deserving extreme penalties, sympathy, on the ground that they were destroyed not for the public good, but to satisfy the cruelty of an individual.

THE SPIRIT OF THE MARTYR

Although the Romans could not understand their way of living and treated them severely, the Christians remained true to their faith. They proved to the world that the Christ life could be lived, no matter what the odds might be. A beautiful account of real Christian living is given in the "Epistle to Diognetus," which was written some time during the persecutions by an anonymous writer:

The Christians are distinguished from other men neither by country, nor language, nor the customs which they observe. . . . Every foreign country is to them as their native land, and every land of their birth as a land of strangers. They marry as do all; they beget children; but they do not commit abortion. They have a common table, but not a common bed. They are in the flesh, but they do not live after the flesh. They pass their days on earth, but they are the citizens of heaven. They obey the prescribed laws, and at the same time surpass the laws by their lives. They love all men, and are persecuted by all. They are unknown and condemned; they are put to death and restored to life. They are poor, yet they make many rich; they are in lack of all things, and yet abound in all. They are dishonored, and yet in their very dishonor are glorified.

They are evil-spoken of, and yet are justified. They are reviled and bless; they are insulted and repay insult with honor; they do good, yet are punished as evil-doers. When punished they rejoice as if quickened into life; they are assailed by the Jews as foreigners and are persecuted by the Greeks; yet those who hate them are unable to assign a reason for their hatred.

Such living makes us want to sing with George Eliot:

> Oh, may I join the choir invisible
> Of those immortal dead who live again
> In minds made better by their presence; live
> In pulses stirred to generosity,
> In deeds of daring rectitude, in scorn
> Of miserable aims that end with self,
> In thoughts sublime that pierce the night like stars,
> And with their mild persistence urge men's search
> To vaster issues.

A Wonderful Letter

Ignatius, the bishop of Antioch in Syria, was arrested and sentenced to be conducted to Rome, where he was to be thrown to the beasts in the arena. The account of this journey resembles very much that of Paul's last journey to Rome. With chains, guards, and friends, he made a wearisome march across the mountains. Whenever he had time, he would write a letter to some friend or church. These letters stand in the same class with those which Paul wrote under similar circumstances. This one, the "Epistle to the Romans," is worth careful study, for it reveals the spirit of the Christians of this period:

I write to all the churches and impress on all, that I shall willingly die for God unless ye hinder me. I beseech you not to show unreasonable good-will toward me. Permit me to be the food of wild beasts, through whom it will be granted me to attain unto God. I am the wheat of God and I am ground by the teeth of wild beasts, that I may be found the pure bread of Christ. Rather entice the wild beasts, that they may become my tomb and leave nothing of my body, so that when I have fallen asleep I may be burdensome to no one. Then I shall be truly a disciple of Jesus Christ, when

the world sees not my body. Entreat Christ for me, that by these
instruments I may be found a sacrifice to God. Not as Peter and
Paul do I issue commandments unto you. They were Apostles, I a
condemned man; they were free, I even until now a slave. But if
I suffer, I shall be the freedman of Jesus Christ, and shall rise
again free in him. And now, being in bonds, I learn not to desire
anything.

"The Scilitan Martyrs," A Drama of Death

Place: Judgment hall at Carthage.

Time: July 17, 180 A.D.

Characters: Saturninus, the proconsul. Speratus, Nartzalus, Cittinus, Donata, Secunda, and Vestia—Christians from Scili, a small
city in northwestern Africa. Herald.

Scene: Six Christians are brought into the judgment hall at
Carthage by some Roman soldiers and are placed before Saturninus,
the proconsul, for judgment.

(*The conversation which follows is as recorded in a writing of the
time of this persecution and forms a fine basis for a one-act play.*)

SATURNINUS: Ye can win the indulgence of our lord the Emperor
   if ye return to a sound mind.

SPERATUS: We have never done ill; we have not lent ourselves to
   wrong; we have never spoken ill; but when we have received ill
   we have given thanks, because we pay heed to our Emperor.

SATURNINUS: We, too, are religious, and our religion is simple;
   and we swear by the genius of our lord the Emperor, and pray
   for his welfare, which also ye too, ought to do.

SPERATUS: If thou wilt peaceably lend me thine ears, I will tell
   thee the mystery of simplicity.

SATURNINUS: I will not lend my ears to thee, when thou beginnest
   to speak evil things of our sacred rites; but rather do thou swear
   by the genius of our lord the Emperor.

SPERATUS: The empire of this world I know not; but rather I
   serve that God whom no man hath seen nor with these eyes can
   see (*1 Tim. 6: 16*). I have committed no theft: but if I have
   bought anything I pay the tax; because I know my Lord, the
   King of kings and Emperor of all nations.

SATURNINUS *to the rest:*   Cease to be of this persuasion.

SPERATUS: It is an ill persuasion to do murder, to bear false witness.

SATURNINUS: Be not partakers of this folly.

CITTINUS: We have none other to fear except only our Lord God, who is in the heaven.

DONATA: Honor to Cæsar as Cæsar, but fear to God.

VESTIA: I am a Christian.

SECUNDA: What I am that I wish to be.

SATURNINUS *to Speratus:* Dost thou persist in being a Christian?

SPERATUS: I am a Christian. (*And with him they all agreed.*)

SATURNINUS: Will ye have a space to consider?

SPERATUS: In a matter so just there is no considering.

SATURNINUS: What are these things in your chest?

SPERATUS: Books and epistles of Paul, a just man.

SATURNINUS: Have a delay of thirty days and bethink yourselves.

SPERATUS: I am a Christian. (*And with him all agreed.*)

SATURNINUS *reading out the decree from the tablet:* "Speratus, Nartzalus, Cittinus, Donata, Vestia, Secunda, and the rest who have confessed that they live according to the Christian rite, because an opportunity has been offered them on returning to the custom of the Romans and they have obstinately persisted, it is determined shall be put to the sword."

SPERATUS: We give thanks to God.

NARTZALUS: Today we are martyrs in heaven; thanks be to God.

SATURNINUS, *ordering it to be proclaimed by the herald:* Speratus, Nartzalus, Cittinus, Veturius, Felix, Aquilinus, Laetatius, Januaria, Generosa, Vestia, Donata, and Secunda I have ordered to be executed.

ALL: Thanks be to God.

.   .   .   .

And so they all at one time were crowned with martyrdom; and they reign with the Father and the Son and the Holy Ghost, forever and ever. Amen.

THE RESULTS OF THE PERSECUTION

The results of the persecution can be summed up in these six points:

1. It "advertised" Christianity and won sympathy, which caused it to grow.

2. It created an intense devotion among the Christians.

3. It proved the truth of Christianity.

4. It produced efficient organizations and leaders.

5. It produced a group of extraordinary literary defenders, such as the apologists and letter writers.

6. It furnished an example for later persecutions.

HELPS FOR STUDY

Written Work

1. What were the outstanding periods of persecution?

2. Give some of the reasons why the Christians were persecuted.

3. Give an account of the first Christian persecution by the Romans.

4. How did Ignatius's journey to Rome resemble that of Paul's last journey?

5. Give a summary of *The Scilitan Martyrs*.

6. What were the results of the persecution?

Oral Discussion

1. Can the Romans be justified in their persecution of the Christians?

2. Is it possible to be a Christian under any situation?

3. Have Christians today as much devotion to their religion as the early Christians had?

4. Where are people today being persecuted because of their religious beliefs?

Special Assignments

1. Make a careful study of the letter of Ignatius, finding some of his points of character, and then compare it with one of Paul's letters.

2. Make a list of hymns which express the spirit of the martyrs.

3. Think upon this statement: "It is easier to die for a religion than it is to live for it."

·5·

BOOKMAKING
. . . the Literature of the Church

BACKGROUND OF THE NEW TESTAMENT

Dean Brown says of the Bible:

We have here a book which refuses to be ignored. On the basis of its wide currency alone, if it had no other and worthier claims to distinction, it challenges the attention of every man who can read. For centuries it has been "the best seller." . . . It goes without saying that every thoughtful, well-educated man will desire to know something of the contents of this book which has gained such a hold upon the attention of the race.

The New Testament is a very complex library. Many different races and civilizations have contributed to it—Babylonian, Egyptian, Persian, Greek, and Roman. But the most important contributions came from the Hebrews, the Greeks, and the Romans.

The Hebrews gave it the soil on which to grow. They gave the essential doctrines of God, man, sin, and salvation. In fact it is quite impossible to understand the New Testament without a knowledge of the fundamental facts of the Old. There are 275 quotations in the New Testament which are taken from the Old. Mark—the oldest gospel—opens with a quotation from the Old Testament. All the evangelists use many quotations from it. John the Baptist began his ministry with a text taken from Isaiah. Jesus often used the Old Testament, taking his first text from it. Peter used it in his great sermon at

Pentecost. The New Testament is therefore greatly indebted to the Hebrews.

The Romans gave to the New Testament its means of growth —the vine. The fine system of roads, which ran all over the Roman world, gave to Christianity a way to expand and grow in influence. The Roman rule also contributed to the idea of law and order, and its influence especially colors the Book of Revelation.

The Greeks gave to the New Testament its beauty of thought and language—the leaves. The language of the disciples, the Aramaic, was only provincial and was not a fit vehicle to carry the wonderful message of the Master. And so Greek, the universal language of the time, was adopted to carry the universal message around the world. This was tremendously important, for not only did it help the gospel to be understood all over the world, but carried with it Greek associations, implications, and overtones which modified the book itself. "So it forgot the tongue of its birthplace and learned the speech of its new motherland." With the new language came a new outlook, a larger mental horizon.

COLLECTING MATERIAL

Jesus did not leave a single written word behind him. He thought very little about books. He never went to graduate school or theological seminary. He seemed to be very content to let his beautiful sayings and stories perish, if only he could see them spring to life again in the hearts of his followers. He did not ask his disciples to "remember" his words, but to "do" them.

Although Jesus put no special emphasis on his sayings in themselves, his disciples memorized many of them word for word. This was quite a natural thing for them to do, for it was in harmony with the customs of their race. One of their proverbs says that "a good pupil is like a cistern lined with mortar, from which not a drop of water can leak out." Jesus, the Great Teacher, had many such pupils, and he made his teachings so clear that they were very easy to remember. Many were the proverbs and stories that he used. And what stories he told! They were perfect! All of his figures of speech were homely and very striking. Nearly all of his sayings were of a poetic nature which made them easy to remember. No doubt at the end of the day his disciples would repeat these words, one to another, as they talked over the acts of their Master for that day.

As time went on after Jesus' death, it was thought wise to write down some of his sayings for those who had no adequate oral record. The earliest of these documents, as far as can be found out, is now contained in the Gospels of Matthew and Luke, being used as one of their sources. It contains a collection of Jesus' sayings, such as the Sermon on the Mount, the parables, and friendly advice given to his disciples. This document today is known by the title, *The Sayings of Jesus,* or *Q*, which stands for the German word "source." It was written in the fifties or early sixties of the first century at Jerusalem. Many think that it was written by the disciple Matthew.

THE FIRST NEW TESTAMENT AUTHOR

Paul was a busy man. Along with all his missionary journeys, he carried on the trade of tentmaking. As time went on situations arose which called forth letters from the hand of Paul—letters of thanks, instruction or advice, criticism, comfort, inspiration, and recommendation. They were often written in haste to serve a very immediate and pressing need. They were not intended for publication, but to serve the needs of a few of his friends or of some church. These letters were usually sent by one of his assistants or by some messengers whom he could secure. In this way, he was able to keep in constant touch with the churches which he had established.

But soon these letters of Paul were copied and sent to some of the other churches (Colossians 4: 16). The original copy was saved by the addressed person or church because it bore the greetings and signature of Paul himself. In this way, therefore, the letters were preserved for future use and so found a place

among the New Testament writings. These letters were written
some time between 50 and 64 A.D. Goodspeed lists them in the
following order: I Thessalonians, II Thessalonians, Galatians,
I Corinthians, II Corinthians, Romans, Philemon, Philippians,
Colossians, and Ephesians. The last three are called "the prison
epistles."

"The Greatest Story Ever Told"

The Gospels are four different stories of the "Greatest Life
Ever Lived." Each story is written by a different author and
with a different purpose in view. We cannot expect them,
therefore, to agree in every detail. Yet there is a strong bond
of unity in all of them: the fact of Jesus Christ. He is the hero
of each of the four stories and the inspiration of each writer.

The title, "The Gospel According to Matthew," does not
necessarily mean that the disciple Matthew was the author of
this story. It is more likely that the writer based his Gospel
upon an account of Matthew's *Sayings of Jesus*, written some
time before this story. The evidence for this is that Papias,
early in the second century, wrote: "Matthew, in the Hebrew
dialect, compiled the Logia, and each one interpreted them
according to his ability."

The point of view and purpose of the story are very plain. He
is writing to the Jews to show that Jesus is the Messiah of the
Old Testament.

The Gospel of Mark was the first story to be written of the
Christ. Matthew and Luke based much of their stories upon
Mark. Papias, writing about 125 A.D., says concerning this
book:

Mark having become the interpreter of Peter, wrote down ac-
curately everything that he remembered, without, however, record-
ing in order what was either said or done by Christ. For neither
did he hear the Lord nor did he follow him; but afterwards, as I
said, Peter, who adapted his instruction to the needs of his hearers
had no design of giving a connected account of the Lord's oracles.

In Mark, Jesus is the mighty doer. He is the Wonder Worker.

It does not appear that Mark is writing specially for either Jews or Gentiles, but is proclaiming to all believers that Jesus is mighty to save.—SNOWDEN.

Doctor Luke is considered to be the author of "The Gospel of Luke." Irenaeus, writing about 180 A.D. says: "Luke, the companion of Paul, recorded in a book the gospel preached by him." Here we find Jesus as the Great Physician. This gospel is written in a fine style and is very accurate. It contains many parables, some of which use technical medical terms. The writer wished to give to the Gentile world a complete story of the life of Jesus.

There is much evidence which favors John, the beloved disciple of Jesus, as the author of the Fourth Gospel. (However, some modern scholars say that it was probably written by a younger John, companion to the elder disciple.) The writer must have been a philosopher. He was more of a poet than the practical Matthew and the objective Mark and the systematic Luke. His story was a new interpretation of the living Christ. It is one of the most original books ever written—not in subject matter, but in the manner of presentation. It takes us nearer the heart of the Man of Galilee than any other single book. John wished to share the experiences which he received daily from the living Christ. Even today we too can share this love with John, if we will but walk with him through his wonderful book.

BINDING THE BOOKS TOGETHER

The twenty-seven books of the New Testament were all written mostly during 50 to 100 A.D. They are grouped about four important events in history: the evangelization of the Gentile world, the fall of Jerusalem, the Roman persecutions, and the rise of sects. But these twenty-seven books were only a selection made from a very large body of Christian literature. The first time that a list of these twenty-seven books appears together as one unit was in a letter written by Athanasius of Alexandria in 367 A.D. But it was a much later date when they were put under one cover.

It was only when printing was invented that the whole New Testament began to be generally circulated in one volume, in Latin, Greek, German, or English.—GOODSPEED.

These books were selected as a result of common agreement among the churches. They judged them to be genuine and to contain the true facts as they happened in history, given by men who had been inspired by the life and teachings of the Master. There is a marked distinction between these books and those others written during the same period. It must be concluded from the facts that these selected books were the result, not of any infallible divine selection, but of careful human judgment. They speak for themselves, revealing their spiritual inspiration.

The arrangement of the New Testament books is not in the order of their writing but follows a general historical order. As the Gospels tell about the life of Jesus, they naturally come first in order. And as Acts tell about the doings of Jesus' disciples, it naturally comes next. And so on through the whole list. This helps to make somewhat of a connected story of the early days of Christianity.

What is the World's true Bible? 'Tis the highest thought of man.
The thought distilled through ages since the dawn of thought began.
   And each age adds a word thereto, some psalm or promise sweet—
   And the canon is unfinished and forever incomplete—
O'er the chapters that are written long and lovingly we pore—
But the best is yet unwritten, for we grow from more to more.
                      SAM WALTER FOSS

HELPS FOR STUDY

Written Work

1. What contributions did the Hebrews, Romans, and Greeks make to Christianity?

2. Describe the process of collecting material for the making of the New Testament.

3. Why did Paul write letters?

4. What do the four Gospels attempt to do?

5. What are the four periods about which the twenty-seven books of the New Testament are grouped?

Oral Discussion

1. Why do so many people buy the Bible?
2. In what respect is the New Testament an original book?
3. Did Jesus regard his words as important enough to be written down?
4. Of what importance are the letters of Paul?
5. Why do not the four Gospels agree?
6. Why do the new translations take us closer to the original words of Christ?

Special Assignments

1. Tell the story of Jesus' writing in the sand.
2. List the New Testament books according to the date of their writing.
3. Write a thousand-word essay on the importance of the Bible.
4. Estimate what proportion of the Gospels are the very words of Jesus.
5. Write a paper on "Translating the Bible."
6. Show that the Fourth Gospel was not intended for a biography.
7. Show that the Fourth Gospel was an inspired interpretation written by the greatest of all Christian mystics.

·6·

GETTING A NEW SHELL
... *Christianity Adapts Itself*
100-323 A.D.

A religion that cannot meet the deepest longings of restless hearts, that fears freedom of speech, that distrusts social reconstruction, that makes respectability its morality, that would muzzle scientific inquiry will be ignored by a world that has outgrown it.

—SHAILER MATHEWS

Notice how this statement applies throughout this chapter.

WANTED—A TRUE RELIGION

The Greeks and Romans were very religious peoples. They had their many gods and were faithful to them. Paul found this to be quite true, especially at Athens, where they were worshiping an unknown God in order that none of the possible gods might be omitted (Acts 17: 23). They were doing their best to find the true religion which would satisfy their souls. As Ropes says: "Christianity came into a world hungering and thirsting for spiritual religion."

They had their many temples where sacrificing was done, their popular superstitions, their magic, and their many rites. Many different philosophies and sects were developed in order to meet their spiritual longings. Each had its rewards—an easy and sensual life for the present world and a life of peace in the future world. Yet all was vague and uncertain. They stimulated the desire for novelty and spiritual union with God,

44

but could not supply it. Each lacked the appeal of a great personality.

So the Roman people became dissatisfied with their old system of religion because it could not satisfy the highest longings of the soul. They wanted redemption from sin, the feeling of safety, and peace. These elements were to be found in the new religion which they at first hated so much. But after they had found that Christianity was a real force, the religion of truth, their feeling of hatred gave way and many received it. When they found that it satisfied the desires of the heart, they rejoiced, for it led them to the source of the true God.

Victory—Christianity Wins

During this period Christianity made great progress. The persecution had won many converts to the new faith. Although it had no Christian government to protect or foster it, Christianity soon grew into manhood. No one knows the number of Christians at this time, for very few records have been left and these give much too low an estimate of the total number. But after careful investigation it is thought that there must have been between 30,000,000 and 100,000,000. McGlothlin says that "by the end of the period, perhaps as much as one-tenth of the population of the empire was Christian." This shows that Christianity was getting a very strong foothold in the Empire. Pagan Rome was giving way to the new faith.

There is no doubt that Christianity would have gained a victory even if Constantine had not appeared as its champion. It was growing stronger each day, for it was the religion of Truth. Nothing could stop its advance. Christianity has been and always will be a "conquering world religion." Kent gives the following reasons for this:

1. The first reason is historical: Christianity sprang from Judaism, the noblest pre-Christian ethical religion.

2. It appeals to the individual will through both the reason and the emotions.

3. It sets before men a worthy goal.

4. Christianity is the only thoroughly democratic religion known to man.

5. Christianity offers the only satisfactory solution of the problem of evil.

6. Christianity is preëminently a social religion.

7. Christianity wins and transforms men by the influence of personality upon personality. It is a spiritual force emanating from God himself, finding concrete and noblest expression in Jesus.

A COMPROMISE

Principal Jacks, in *The Challenge of Life,* makes this statement:

Nowhere in the Gospels do I find the faintest indication of a "good time coming," either for the individual or the race, when, by the adoption of an appropriate "system" (either of theology or of economics), cross-bearing will be done away and lotus-eating takes its place.

In other words, he says that the Christian life, if it expects to develop heroes, must always be a struggle. Here, in this period of the early Church, is where Christianity made its first great mistake. It stopped fighting, not because it had been defeated, but because it had won the victory. From now on it began to lose its spiritual strength. It began to compromise. "Christianity took, molded, guided, and was itself affected by, the forces which it found already working in human life" (Ropes).

In the first place there was a marked change in Christian belief and doctrine. Christianity began to absorb much of the speculation and superstition of its neighbors. A good example of this is found in the Gnostic school of semi-Christian thought which met the special needs of men trained by centuries in paganism and philosophy. As time goes on, we have to look more and more to these Greek philosophers for the ideas which the Christians developed. This fact explains many of the dark places in Christian writings.

And then there was the great change which began to take place in the organization of the Church. They took Jesus from the fields and lakesides and put him in large buildings full of noisy people. They took his very simple teachings and wove about them so much doctrine that finally they were nearly lost in the attempt to find out what the doctrine meant. The Church soon began to be thought of as a saving institution, outside of which there was no salvation. Its bishops were supposed to be successors of the apostles. The control of the Church was in their hands and the laity lost its power of speech.

This universal Church was believed to be infallibly guided by the Holy Spirit, so that it was kept from error. It was the body of Christ, a holy entity; to rend it was the worst possible sin.

—MC GLOTHLIN

A KING BECOMES A CHRISTIAN

Constantine was born about 274 A.D. at Naissus, in Upper Mœsia. His father, Emperor Claudius, was a great general and became the Cæsar of the West. His mother, Helena, was a Christian, a daughter of an innkeeper. He received most of his education from court circles and the battlefields, which made him, like his father, a great general as well as a good statesman.

At this time the Empire had three rulers: Maxentius and Constantine in the West, and Licinius in the East. In 312 Maxentius began a march on his rival, but when Constantine received the news he at once began a march toward Rome. They met at the Milvian Bridge, just outside Rome, and a fierce battle took place. Constantine finally defeated Maxentius, who was drowned in the Tiber. This gave Constantine full power in the West. A few years later (324) Licinius was defeated; and Constantine became Emperor of the United Roman Empire.

The story of Constantine's conversion to Christianity dates back to this battle at the Milvian Bridge. One day, as tradition tells us, during the conflict with Maxentius, he and his whole army saw a great shining cross before them in the sky with this inscription on it: "In this sign, conquer." That night in a dream the Christ appeared before Constantine and commanded him to use the emblem as a battle ensign, and the result would surely be victory. So he immediately did as the Christ had said and with this new strength vanquished his foe at the Milvian Bridge. From that time on Constantine was a friend of the Christians and did a great deal to establish the Universal Church.

THE STATE-CHURCH

There is no doubt that Constantine's connection with Christianity marks a new epoch in Christian history. It was he who first gave Christianity protection by law. He saw in it a unifying and organizing force and with great insight adopted it as the religion of the Empire. He sought to win the whole Empire to Christianity through the Christian governors in the different provinces. He converted temples into churches and appointed special times and places for worship.

His imperial laws, improving woman's condition, mitigating slavery, abolishing crucifixion as a method of punishment, and caring for the unfortunate, breathe forth the spirit of Christian justice and humanity.—FLICK.

Thus the Christians soon forgot all about their former trials and persecutions, for now they had nothing to fear. They had become a very important part of a great system of government. It was now no longer the Church but the State-Church.

HELPS FOR STUDY

Written Work

1. What type of a religion did the Romans have?
2. Why did the Romans seek a true religion?
3. In what way did Christianity win a victory?
4. Give the reasons why Christianity is a "conquering religion."
5. What compromise did Christianity make?
6. Tell the story of Constantine's conversion.
7. What is meant by the term "State-Church"?

Oral Discussion

1. Was there any good in the religion of the Romans?
2. Is victory always best for a religion, country, etc.?
3. When is a compromise justified?
4. Was Constantine really a Christian according to the standards of Jesus?

Special Assignments

1. Read, in H. G. Wells' *Outline of History,* the account of the progress of Christianity during this period.
2. Write a brief account of the life of Constantine.
3. Make a list of Bible characters who met moral defeat at the time when they were most successful.
4. Explain the meaning of Gnosticism? How did it influence Christianity?

· 7 ·

NO RIVALS
. . . the Undivided Catholic Church
323-600 A.D.

The orignal mistake was made when Christianity borrowed the type of its institutions from the kingdoms that are of this world, the political kingdoms, with which in an evil hour it was persuaded to enter into a most unnatural alliance. To Christianity was given the model of a heavenly city, but instead of bringing that city down to earth, it made for itself an earthly model, and so built the Tower of Babel once more.—PRINCIPAL L. P. JACKS.

WHAT THE STATE DEMANDED OF THE CHURCH

Since the State was the means by which Christianity won its victory, it wished to share in the management of the Church. Now that new power had come to the State, it grew strong once more. Many of the clergy were given high offices in the government. Great sums of money were given for the building of new churches and charity. Everything was done on a large scale. Christianity was made the popular religion of the State.

While, on the surface, it might seem that the Church was free and powerful, yet, at the same time, it was shut fast in a prison made with its own hands. With freedom from persecution came something far worse than the severest persecution, that is, moral decay. Truly, the Church was free from the fears of the sword, but it was not free to rule its own household. It became in too many ways merely a tool for the ambitions of the selfish and immoral rulers of the State. Using it as a tool the State demanded from it:

1. The right to administer ecclesiastical law.
2. The right to call all general councils and to conform their actions.
3. The right to elect all bishops of important sees.
4. The right of supreme judge in the spiritual courts.
5. A deciding vote in all dogmatic controversies.

HEADQUARTERS OF THE STATE-CHURCH

The Church at Rome grew very strong. It was situated at the center of the great empire and at a time when it was the mistress of the world. Paul saw great hopes for this Church of Rome, for it naturally seemed to have great power and influence. But no doubt Paul would have been very disappointed in it if he could have visited it during this period. It had taken on the organization of the Empire, and after the State and Church had become one, it became its servant. Thus the capital of the Empire became the capital of the State-Church. The Pontifex of the Empire merely became the Pope of the State-Church. The government remained the same. The Roman language was adopted and Roman rites, festivities, and ceremonies were used. And so from this powerful city as headquarters, the State-Church began its conquest of the whole world. Here is the beginning of the Roman Catholic Church which has lasted even to this day.

THE RISE OF THE PAPACY

This new system of Church government naturally gave the priest a very high position. He was soon thought of as mediator between God and man. This led to a differentiation of the ministry, which, in turn, developed the hierarchy. The Bishop of Rome became the head of all the other bishops, the chosen representative of God on earth. All of the Church officers, from the lowest to the highest, were separated from the laity by a very wide gulf. As time revealed the perfection of this plan, an hierarchal organization was formed. The Pope was the head of the entire Church; the archbishop was the head of an ecclesiastical province; the bishops were heads of dioceses; the priests were assistants to the bishops in the care of souls; and the deacons were assistants to the priests.

As a result of this, ritualism began to play a large part in worship. Holy water, sacred relics and places, pilgrimages, the use of the cross became evident in the services. Image worship was introduced in the form of saints. Many festivals such as Easter, Pentecost, Epiphany, and various saints' days were added.

PERILS OF THE NEW ORDER

This unnatural union of Church and State had many bad effects upon the true spirit of Christianity. It was now very different from the simple religion which Jesus taught. In organization it was no longer a democracy, but an absolute monarchy. It was now no struggling Church, but a mighty Church of grandeur, a power factor in society, industry, and education.

But as short cuts to success are always unwise, so it was in this case. The object of Christianity was to establish the kingdom of God in the hearts of men. This could be done only step by step, through kindly living and loving service. As Josiah Gilbert Holland says:

> Heaven is not reached by a single bound;
> But we build the ladder by which we rise,
> From lowly earth to the vaulted skies,
> And we mount to its summit round by round.
>
> I count this thing to be grandly true:
> That a noble deed is a step toward God,
> Lifting the soul from the common clod,
> To a purer air and a broader view.

In her great success the Church forgot almost entirely about noble living. This was fatal to her spiritual life. From this period to the Reformation, the Church grew from bad to worse, until finally it was preserved and rescued from its corruption by Martin Luther.

Some of the results of this new order of the State-Church were:

1. A half-converted mass of heathen were added to the Church.

2. The Church became a center for worldiness and secular glory.

3. The Church became the slave of selfish and ambitious statesmen.

4. The Church was limited in its freedom.

CHRISTIANITY IN OTHER LANDS

Meanwhile, Christianity was gaining a strong foothold in other lands outside of the Empire. Yet even in these lands it was under the control of the pope at Rome. Christian missionaries went to Persia, Armenia, Southern Arabia, India, China, and Abyssinia. In the west, Christianity was taken to Spain, France, England, Ireland, Scotland, and Germany. It will not be long before we hear of some of these countries rebelling and demanding that the Church once more return to the religion of Jesus.

HELPS FOR STUDY

Written Work

1. What demands did the State make of the Church?
2. Why did Rome become the headquarters of the Church?
3. Describe the rise of the papacy.
4. What were the bad results of the new order?
5. To what other lands did Christianity spread?

Oral Discussion

1. Did the Church make a mistake by accepting the same form of organization as that of the Empire?
2. Why did the Church grow corrupt?
3. Can an institution save people?
4. What good is there in ritualism?
5. In what countries is the Church in most danger of losing its freedom?

Special Assignments

1. Make a chart showing the relation of the Church to the State during this period.

2. Describe the elements needed in a church building to promote worship.

3. Write a paper on "The Value of a Protestant Confessional."

4. Discover what is involved in our practice of the separation of Church and State.

·8·

THE CHURCH OF CREEDS
. . . the Church as a System of Doctrine, 325-800 A.D.

The defence of religion has been overdone. We have cooped up the faith in theological fortresses, surrounding it with an immense array of outworks—creeds, dogmas, apologetics, institutions—and we have used up our resources in holding our positions against one another when we ought to have been attacking the common enemy in the open field. These outworks and defences, intended to save us from perplexity, have become a greater source of perplexity than all the rest. It takes a lifetime to understand them, and when understood most of them turn out futile.—PRINCIPAL L. P. JACKS.

WHY THE CHURCH NEEDED CREEDS

This period was the great age of creedmaking. All Christians at this time were interested in theology, and they discussed and defined the most difficult doctrines. Gregory of Nyssa, speaking of the Arian controversy in Constantinople, said:

Everything in the city is full of such (as dogmatizing over things incomprehensible),—the lanes, the markets, the avenues, the streets, the cloisters, the bankers, the dealers in provisions. When you ask one how much a thing costs, he will favor you with a discourse about the begotten and the unbegotten. When you inquire the price of bread, he replies: "The Father is greater than the Son, and the Son is subordinate." If you ask: "Is the bath ready?" he declares: "The Son was created from nothing." I know not by what name, whether frenzy or madness or other kindred terms, this evil which has come upon the people may fitly be called.

As a result of this, there rose up within the Church many different parties, each giving a different interpretation to the same doctrine. This led to theological struggles which were so bitterly fought that blood was shed, bishops were banished, and empires shook with fear.

Now what was the need of all this commotion? The answer is this: Since Jesus left no definite creed upon which all Christians might agree, it was necessary for them to think out for themselves just what to believe and what not to believe, in order that they might be able to stand on common ground. Now this was a hard thing to do, for all were not ready to accept what the other believed. Yet something had to be done, since it was necessary to have some form of belief to take the place of dying paganism.

And so the controversy went on, until it came to be centered around a very fine point—the divinity of Christ. On one side stood Arius, while on the other side stood Athanasius. Now the battle is on, but few get killed. Most of the powder is used up in making a great noise with blank cartridges and fireworks. They make many marches; they seldom meet in close combat. Yet many get badly hurt with their own weapons. They are very poor soldiers.

Constantine soon realized that this was not good for the political situation of the Empire. He took direct measures, therefore, to stop this war of words. First, he asked them to sign a peace treaty, but they would not hear to that. Next, he called together the "Generals" and "Captains" of the "Army" in order that they might draw up a compromise, in the form of a creed, on which they both could agree. As a result of this council, the Nicene Creed was formed—a statement of doctrine which has lasted even to the present day.

THE FIRST CHRISTIAN CREED

The first Christian creed actually dates back to an earlier period (200 A.D.), although it was not put in formal written usage until the fourth or fifth century. It is called the "Apostles' Creed," yet it was not written by the apostles; nor was it the work of a council, as was the Nicene Creed. As the Christian missionaries went from place to place, it was necessary for them to have some statement of faith which the converts could agree to before they received baptism. This statement of belief was commonly used and has come to be the most widely used statement of the Christian faith that has ever been developed. Today millions accept it to express their own faith. It is as follows:

I believe in God the Father Almighty, Maker of Heaven and Earth;
And in Jesus Christ His only Son our Lord:
Who was conceived by the Holy Ghost, Born of the Virgin Mary:
Suffered under Pontius Pilate, Was crucified, dead, and buried: He descended into Hell;
The third day He arose from the dead:
He ascended into Heaven, and sitteth on the right hand of God, the Father Almighty:
From thence He shall come to judge the quick and the dead.
I believe in the Holy Ghost:
The Holy Catholic Church; the Communion of Saints:
The Forgiveness of sins:
The Resurrection of the body;
And the Life everlasting.   Amen.

The Battle of Words

The Council of Nicæa took place in the year 325 A.D. It was the first universal council of the Christian Church. There were about two thousand present, of whom more than three hundred were bishops. All the provinces of the empire were represented, except Britain; yet only six delegates were sent from the West. As the Pope was too old to attend in person he sent two presbyters to take his place.

In the first part of the council the Arians had the advantage, since Constantia, the sister of the Emperor, and many learned men were on their side. But when Arius presented his creed it created such an uproar that it was seized and torn to pieces along with his doctrines. At that moment Eusebius of Cæsarea came forward with an old Palestine creed which he proposed as a compromise, and it would have been accepted as it stood, had not Athanasius objected. After two months of debate it was finally accepted as revised, although Eusebius himself hesitated to sign it, for great was the change. But the Emperor favored it and compelled all bishops to subscribe to it.

Now that business of the council was finished, Arius was publicly excommunicated and a splendid feast was given the delegates by Constantine. It was so wonderful that Eusebius likened it to the kingdom of heaven.

The Nicene Creed

The adoption of the Nicene Creed was a marvelous intellectual and spiritual feast. The doctrines, as found in this creed, have stood throughout the ages. All of the great creeds of later dates have been based upon this first universal Christian creed. Because of its great importance in Christian history, it is given here in its original form:

We believe in one God, the Father Almighty, Maker of all things, both visible and invisible. And in one Lord Jesus Christ,
   the Son of God.
Begotten of the Father, an only-begotten—that is, from the essence (*ousia*) of the Father—
      God from God,
      Light from Light,
      True God from true God,
begotten, not made,
      being of one essence (*Homoousion*) with the Father;
by whom all things were made,
      both things in heaven and things on earth:
who for us men and for our salvation came down and was made flesh,
      was made man, suffered, and rose again the third day,
      ascended into heaven,
      cometh to judge the quick and the dead;
And in the Holy Spirit.
   But those who say that
      there was once when he was not; and
      before he was begotten he was not; and

he was made of things that were not;
or maintain that the Son of God is of a different essence (*hypostasis* or *ousia*) or created or subject to moral change or alteration —these doth the Catholic and Apostolic Church anathematize.

THE RESULTS OF CONTROVERSY

This, then, was the age when standards of orthodoxy concerning both God and Christ were fixed. To a great extent they have held to the present time, although perhaps they have been changed somewhat in their outward form in order to meet the needs of the time. These great controversies and the Nicene Creed, therefore, had far-reaching results. Some of the results were:

1. The Church was given its first written creed which became the basis of all later creeds.

2. Church canons were established.

3. The date for Easter was determined.

4. The pope was recognized as the only head of the Church.

5. The Council of Nicæa marked the beginning of the breach between Eastern and Western Churches.

6. The State was given a final vote in all vital concerns of the Church.

7. Various heresies and schisms of the time were condemned.

8. The Nestorians, Armenians, and several smaller bodies severed from and still remain apart from the Catholic Church.

AN IDEAL CREED

I believe in the Fatherhood of God;
I believe in the words of Jesus;
I believe in the clean heart;
I believe in the service of love;
I believe in the unworldly life;
I believe in the Beatitudes;
I promise to trust God and follow Christ,
To forgive my enemies and to seek after the righteousness of God.—JOHN WATSON.

HELPS FOR STUDY

Written Work

1. Why did the Church need a creed?
2. Why did Constantine want the Church to have a creed?
3. What was the Apostles' Creed first used for?
4. What happened at the Council of Nicæa?
5. Give five results of the controversy.

Oral Discussion

1. Should the Church of today adopt a creed?
2. Would Jesus accept the Nicene Creed?
3. Should every person have a creed?
4. How can we have any measure of real Christian unity as long as there are so many different doctrines?

Special Assignments

1. Using the Sermon on the Mount as a source, make what would seem to be Jesus' creed.
2. Compare in detail the Apostles' Creed and the Nicene Creed.
3. Make a collection of poems which will give examples of the many different creeds of people.
4. Discover who the Apologists were.
5. Comment upon the following statement:

"What the Church said, in effect, was that neither Arianism nor Apollinarianism nor Nestorianism nor Eutychianism would do, and that, apart from the negative, the orthodox doctrine was sufficiently contained in the Nicene Creed."—A. E. J. RAWLINSON.

·9·

THE CHURCH OF CORRUPTION
. . . the Church of the Middle Ages
600-1500 A.D.

It is frequently said that Europe in the sixth and seventh centuries relapsed into barbarism, but that does not express the reality of the case. It is far more correct to say that the civilization of the Roman Empire had passed into a phase of extreme demoralization. Barbarism is a social order of an elementary type, orderly within its limits; but the state of Europe beneath its political fragmentation was a social disorder. Its morale was not that of a kraal, but that of a slum. For in a savage kraal a savage knows that he belongs to a community, and lives and acts accordingly; in a slum, the individual within neither knows of nor acts in relation to any greater being.—H. G. WELLS.

THE COMING OF THE BARBARIANS

As early as 375 A.D., the people from the north began to migrate and invade the Roman Empire. In 476 the line of western emperors came to an end. At the opening of the sixth century the Ostrogoths had settled in Italy, the Franks in Gaul, the Anglo-Saxons in Britain, the Visigoths in Spain, and the Vandals in northern Africa.

It was the Frankish king, Clovis, who laid the foundation for what afterward became the empire of Charles the Great. He, like most of the invaders, became a Christian, and as a result of this a close relationship between the Church and the Frankish dominions was formed. Although for a while after the death of Clovis conditions sank to a very low ebb, they were revived again under Pippin (687). His son, Charles Martel (715 to 741), for political reasons, greatly aided the Church and promoted many missionary and reformatory works in western Germany. When the Lombards began their invasion of Italy, the Pope called on Charles Martel for aid, but all was in vain. So the Pope crowned Pippin the Short (754), who had been wanting this kingly title, and with the aid of this general the Lombards were defeated and Rome saved. Thus began the Holy Roman Empire, which played so big a part in medieval history.

At the death of Pippin the Short in 768, his kingdom was divided between his two sons, Charles and Carloman. In 771 Carloman died and the entire kingdom was left in the hands of Charles. This sovereign was far ahead of his age. Not only was he a great general, but also

. . . the patron of learning, the kindly master of the Church, the preserver of order, to whom nothing seemed too small for attention or too great for execution.—WALKER.

His sway ruled what is now the countries of France, Belgium, Holland, and nearly half of Germany, Austria, Hungary, and Italy. He was so great that the world has added the word "great" to his name, thus making it—Charlemagne.

THE STATE OF GOD

It was through Charlemagne that the old line of Roman Cæsars was revived in Europe. The Roman Empire had died at the hands of the invaders from the north and the Byzantine Empire of the East had gone far into decline. But the Roman Church still lived on. The Pope still had the title of "Pontifex Maximus" and was not ready yet to give it up.

Christianity at this stage had lost most of its vision of the kingdom of Heaven, for it was greatly blinded by its task of reviving the Roman ascendancy which it thought of as its inheritance. As a result of this, it had become a political body which used its members to further its material ends.

It was quite natural that Charlemagne should be willing to

receive the crown at the hands of the Pope. For many years there had been a firm alliance between the Pope and Charlemagne's predecessors. Each had received mutual benefit from it. Now at this time, both Charlemagne and the Pope had an idea of a great Holy Roman Empire where each would have world-wide dominion, each supreme within his own sphere.

And so, on December 25, 800 A.D., as Charlemagne was kneeling in prayer at Rome, the Pope advanced and placed a crown upon his head, thus restoring once again the line of Roman "Cæsars." At this point begins the struggle between Pope and empire which lasted all through the Middle Ages.

The Papacy Grows Strong

During the period following the death of Charlemagne, there was a rapid decline in the empire. His son, Louis the Pious, was wholly unfit for the task left by Charlemagne. His sons plotted against him and, at his death, the empire was divided between them by the Treaty of Verdun in 843. As the empire thus declined, the papacy grew in power. The popes showed themselves the strongest men of the time. The papacy was now the only well-organized system of government in the Middle Ages. Everything had to bow before it.

As a result of feudalism the Church received great amounts of land and money. As its wealth increased, it became more and more powerful, until finally

. . . by utilizing the vast ecclesiastical power already attained, [it was able] to exert a controlling influence in civil matters, and even to set up and depose kings and emperors.—NEWMAN.

At this period the Church was present absolutely everywhere. It entered every home, it controlled the government, it was the guest at every board, it blessed or refused to bless every new-born babe, it taught every growing child, it regulated marriage and the rights of burial. It had control of the conscience of the confessional and money through penance. It offered or withheld as it pleased the soul's peace while upon earth, and its salvation in eternity. One could not have escaped the Church no matter how hard he tried.

SINS OF THE CHURCH

The degradation and pollution of the Church at this time are too extreme to be put into words. The whole situation has been described as:

. . . an Augean stable in which adultery and theft were among the virtues of an age addicted to more abominable and unnatural crimes. The iniquities of that time must be concealed in Latin; society today would not tolerate their translation.

The monks and priests had yielded to the temptation of wealth and luxury. As the Latin language was alone used in connection with the Church, the mass of the people in the Germanic lands were totally ignorant of the Bible and the ideals of it. It was believed that the blessing of God could be purchased by gifts of money, and this belief was worked to its fullest degree by the selfish priests. Thus the system of indulgences was established. This permitted the people to make certain payments in order to be relieved from the punishment of committed sins.

As the priests were not of the highest spiritual type and sometimes quite ignorant, conditions grew to be very serious. Finally some of the higher-minded laity and clergy did rise up in rebellion against such actions. They were the preservers of society during these dark ages. If it had not been for these few, who still held to the true and the beautiful, real Christianity would have been lost during this period (see Chapter XI).

DEFECTIVE PIETY

As the Church lost its spiritual vision and purity, it sought to cover up its sins by the use of outward and physical forms. There developed, therefore, at this time such manifestations as penances, indulgences, masses for the dead, ordeals, pilgrimages, and confessions. But they were only dead forms, invented to take the place of the slower and the harder way to salvation. The freshness and saving power of the Master's spirit was not contained in them. They knew him not.

But we should not think that all the Christians of this period were hopeless. There were many noble men in the Church, but they were overpowered. Soon we are to study the lives of some of these men who helped to keep vital Christianity alive when the world was covered with the shadow of sin and death.

> Like you this Christianity or not?
> It may be false, but will you wish it true?
> Has it your vote to be so if it can?
>
> BROWNING

HELPS FOR STUDY

Written Work

1. Give a brief summary of the invasion of the barbarians.
2. What does the term "State of God" mean?
3. What gave the papacy such great strength?
4. Describe the moral condition of the Church during this period.
5. What were some of the forms of worship at this time?

Oral Discussion

1. What made Christianity appeal to the barbarians?
2. Is it possible to have two absolute controls to any organization?
3. Does the end always justify the means used in Christian work?
4. What are the sins of the Church today?
5. Does it ever pay to pretend?

Special Assignments

1. Draw a map showing the countries under the control of the pope during this period.
2. Write a brief account of the life of Charlemagne.
3. Learn something about Alcuin.
4. Read Plutarch's *Lives* for information concerning some of the Church fathers.

· 10 ·

CLEAN GARMENTS
. . . the Growth of Monasticism

TYPES OF MONASTICISM IN OTHER RELIGIONS

Centuries before the Christian era many so-called heathen religions had certain forms of monastic life. The sacred writings of the Hindus reveal many stories dealing with the lives of holy hermits. It was their belief that, in order to obtain salvation, it was necessary to pray much and to make many personal sacrifices. In Jainism (a religion of India) Mahavira, its founder, lived the life of a hermit monk. For twelve years he wandered about, being injured by wild beasts and men, and undergoing terrible self-imposed bodily suffering. Prince Gautama, the founder of Buddhism, also lived the life of an ascetic. At twenty-nine he left his wife, a new-born son, and the inheritance to the throne to become a monk. He endured much privation and mental suffering until the age of thirty-five. Then one night, while sitting under a bo-tree, he received a great enlightenment. The greatest good in Buddhism is to be able to enter into Nirvana—a state of pure nothingness. Judaism has its examples of a rugged type of ascetism in such characters as Elijah, Elisha, Samuel, and John the Baptist. Greece and Rome had their form of ascetic living in order to produce the ideal life. So monasticism was not new with the Christian religion.

HERMITS OF THE EAST

At the very center of monasticism was the desire to gain the

67

ideal life. The true monk wished to get away from the wicked world and find peace with God through meditation and prayer. As the peoples of the East are much given to reflection, it was quite natural that a great many of them would want to go apart from the superficial world into the quiet places of the desert. Here they would escape the many distractions of everyday life, subordinate their body as they pleased, and dream of the beauties of the future life. Their chief aim was to live in order to die. The climate was suited to this type of life and the hermits increased in great numbers, especially in Egypt.

The first Christian hermit of note was Anthony (251 to 356) who lived in Koma, in Central Egypt. His call came one day when he was at church and heard the story of Jesus and the rich young ruler. He was so impressed with the words of Jesus that he sold his estate for the benefit of the poor, gave his sister to a group of virgins, and went into the desert to be a hermit. Here he practiced self-denial in its hardest forms and gained so great a fame that many came to visit him. Soon he had many imitators, some living alone, and some in groups. There existed no organization or rule, the converts devising their own forms of worship and self-denial. The practices of self-torture were many. Some wore hair shirts, carried heavy weights, slept in thorn bushes; others lived for years on the top of a pillar or in cramped quarters. Many never washed their bodies nor cared for their hair, teeth, and nails. St. Abraham did not wash his face for fifty years, yet his biographer proudly writes: "His face reflected the purity of his soul." Cleanliness was a sign of sin, while dirt was next to godliness.

Back of this desire to flee from the world, and to seek God in a personal way, were the following reasons which are the result of the customs and thinking of that age:

1. A false understanding of the teachings of Jesus.
2. The belief that matter was the seat of all evil.
3. Increasing worldliness of the Church.
4. The feeling of uselessness of living in a world of violence.

THE FIRST CHRISTIAN MONASTERY

It was Pachomius (282 to 346), a converted heathen soldier, who created the first monastic order and organized the first Christian monastery (322) at Tabenna on the Nile. Here the monks lived in a single body, had organized work, regular hours of worship, and were under the control of an abbot. Once a day they met in silence for a common meal. They all wore hoods so that they could not be recognized. Prayer was held thirty-six times daily and a part of the day was given over to manual labor. This type of monasticism was relatively wholesome, so much so that a convent was established at Tabenna for women. By 346 there were ten monasteries in Egypt and, by the end of the fourth century, they spread to nearly every province in the Roman Empire.

MONASTICISM COMES WEST

Monasticism in the East and monasticism in the West were not the same thing. Although both had the same fundamental reason for living apart from the world—to escape the wickedness of the world and the Church—yet they differed greatly in their mode of living. Instead of being of the meditative type, the Western monk was in the main a practical man, active in the affairs of the world. He believed in making the world better by living in it. The Western monks, therefore, became leaders in all the great reforms of the day and played an important part in politics.

The introduction of monasticism into the West resulted very largely from Athanasius' *Life of Anthony*. Also Jerome, Ambrose, and Augustine did much to bring it into favor. The earliest monks were laymen, but later Eusebius, Bishop of Vercelli, in Italy, began the practice of requiring the clergy of his cathedral to live in the monasteries. This led to the priestly ordination of monks.

At one time there were 37,000 monasteries in the West. They produced 24 popes, 200 cardinals, 4,000 bishops, 55,505 saints and 16,000 distinguished writers. The two greatest orders of the time were the Franciscans, founded by Francis of Assisi

(1213), and the Dominicans, founded by Dominic, a Spanish noble, in 1216. These two orders played a very important part all through Europe during the Middle Ages.

THE RULE OF ST. BENEDICT

The greatest organizer of Western monasticism was Benedict. He was born of rich parents and was sent to Rome to be educated. But he became disgusted with the morals of his time, left college, and at sixteen retired to a cave about thirty miles from Rome. Here he became a severe ascetic, choosing "to be ignorant and holy rather than educated and wicked." Soon he attracted many by his mode of living and many disciples were made. He then established twelve monasteries, making the one at Monte Cassino central.

In order to control these monasteries Benedict drew up in 529 what is called the "Holy Rule." It consisted of twenty-three chapters which dealt with social, moral, liturgical, and penal subjects. It provided a monarchial organization with a democratic spirit. An abbot, appointed for life by the monks, ruled the monastery. He had certain assistants called priors, who were elected on their merit. A year of probation was required before a new monk could be elected. Outside of regular hours for study and meditation were periods of manual labor. Indolence was the worst sin and obedience the chief virtue.

This system spread slowly over Europe and was carried as far north as England by missionaries. It was supported by the best men of the Middle Ages and the Church encouraged and favored it. Thus it grew to be a great power.

THE MONK AS THE IDEAL MAN

As the monastery came into prominence through the Church and politics, it invited to its fold those people in whom the spirit of adventure ran the highest. The monks were thus the bold men of the age. They were the leaders and patterns to be followed above all others. Every father desired to see his son enter the monastic life. It became the center of attraction for those who were anxious and ambitious to gain literary attainments. Every young noble saw in it his chance to gain political glory. Every priest saw in it a chance to become a prior or an abbot. In fact the monastery held splendid hopes for all those who were red-blooded and wanted to enter into a great adventure.

The following statement by Montalembert shows to how great a height the officials of the monasteries rose. (It can also be applied to the abbots as well as to the abbesses.)

The abbesses, as we have seen by the example of Hilda, Ebba, and Elfleda, had soon an authority and influence which rivalled that of the most venerated bishops and abbots. They had often the retinue and state of princesses, especially when they came from royal blood. They were treated with kings, bishops, and the greatest lords on terms of perfect equality; and as the rule of the cloister does not seem to have existed for them, they are to be seen going where they pleased, present at all great religious and national solemnities, at the dedication of churches, and even, like queens, taking part in the deliberations of the nations' assemblies and affixing their signatures to the charters therein granted.

THE SALT OF CIVILIZATION

The monks were the principal conservators of the religion and civilization of the Middle Ages. They were excelled by none as the conservators of learning. It was their practice to copy the old manuscripts of former ages, especially those of the Greeks and the Romans; they recorded the thought and progress of their own day; indeed, they were the schoolmasters of their times and through their missionary zeal many of the barbarian tribes were made Christian. They were the champions of orthodoxy in religion, the promoters of higher ideals, humility and purity, friends to the poor, both in a material and in a spiritual sense.

It was always the monks who saved the Church from sinking, emancipated her when becoming enslaved to the world, defended her when assailed.—HARNACK.

In a social way they helped to mitigate the terrors of slavery and to establish the ideals of peace, obedience, purity, and charity. In a political way they supplied the best statesmen, promoted democracy, held back the barbarians, and saved the important vassals. In an educational way they developed musicians, painters, sculptors, architects, and education; built schools, universities, and churches. These all helped industrially, for such things gave work to many hands.

WHY MONASTICISM DID NOT LAST

The monastic orders finally became very rich and powerful. Great amounts of land had been given them by kings and nobles. The abbots grew into secular lords, who fought at the head of troops, went hunting, and entered into the joys of the world. Too much emphasis was placed upon works, making religion too formal. A false conception of hell and judgment caused undue superstition. Family ties were broken down and the state of marriage was lowered. Patriotism was forgotten. The monks became corrupt in their moral life. Everything, in general, became sordid and increasingly corrupt.

But monasticism had filled its place in the world and had filled it well. All of its evils were nothing compared with its good. It passed away as a new age dawned, because it was not adapted to cope with the spirit of the new era. It had lived its natural life, leaving behind such treasures as would enrich all future ages.

> Nothing that is shall perish utterly,
> But perish only to revive again
> In other forms—as clouds restore in rain
> The exhalations of the earth and sea.
> Men build their houses from the masonry
> Of ruined tombs; the passion and the pain
> Of hearts that long have ceased to beat
> Remain, and throb in hearts that are, or are to be.
>
> From *The Daily Altar*

HELPS FOR STUDY

Written Work

1. How did monasticism express itself in other religions?
2. Why did monasticism develop so favorably in the East?
3. Describe the first Christian monastery.
4. How did the monasteries of the East and West differ?
5. Give the fundamental rules of St. Benedict.
6. Why was the monk an ideal man?
7. What was the value of monasticism?
8. Why could the monasteries not last?

Oral Discussion

1. When is a person truly religious?
2. What have we yet to learn from the East?
3. Which type of monasticism was the better—that of the East, or that of the West?
4. In your mind, who is an ideal Christian?
5. In what way should a Christian be separate from the world?
6. Is there, at the present time, a need for a deeper expression in the Christian life?

Special Assignments

1. Make a list of all the requirements that Jesus laid down for his followers. How should they be interpreted?
2. Sketch the life of St. Francis.
3. Sketch the life of St. Bernard.

11

LIGHTS IN THE DARKNESS
. . . Great Christians of the Dark Ages, 260-1153 A.D.

"Biography is the only true history," says Carlyle. Each age or nation is molded in the form of its greatest men. Their ideals stand to a great extent for longings of the masses. No nation can be any greater than its leaders. And so it is with the Church. "By its leaders thou shalt know it." Let us take a look at the Church, therefore, through the lives of some of its greatest leaders and perhaps we, too, can learn the elements of character which made them great, and thus be able to apply new ideas to our own living.

> Lives of great men all remind us
>   We can make our lives sublime,
> And, departing, leave behind us,
>   Footprints on the sands of time.
> Footprints, that perhaps another,
>   Sailing o'er life's solemn main,
> A forlorn and shipwrecked brother,
>   Seeing, shall take heart again.
>
> LONGFELLOW

EUSEBIUS, THE FIRST CHURCH HISTORIAN

Eusebius of Cæsarea was born about 260 A.D., in the land of Palestine. He was educated in the schools of Antioch and Cæsarea. After teaching a few years in the theological school at Cæsarea, he traveled in Egypt and on his return became a bishop. During the Council of Nicæa, Eusebius played a very important part by taking his stand on the middle ground, although tending somewhat toward the left. But he was a man of peace and moderation, not willing to start any trouble. He was temperate, impartial, and truth-loving—rare virtues for the times in which he lived.

Eusebius was more of a learned collector than an elegant writer or critical student. His *Chronicle* is a remarkable book of history. It is an outline of universal history up until 325 A.D. It was so well done that for centuries no historian attempted to write on that period, for it was thought that Eusebius had said all that could be said. Without knowing it, he founded a school of church historians who have given us many valuable accounts of the events which happened from the age of Constantine until 600 A.D.

Some of his works are: *Life and Eulogy* (of Constantine), *Theophany, Upon the Church, Theology, Some Commentaries* (on the Bible), and writings on *Biblical Introduction and Archæology.*

ATHANASIUS, THE FATHER OF ORTHODOXY

If Constantine was called "The Great," Athanasius should be called "The Greater." He was a fighter and conqueror on the battlefields of intellectualism and morality, fighting against error and even the imperial courts.

It was on a Martyr's Day, 313, that Bishop Alexander of Alexandria walked down the street and noticed some small boys playing at imitating a church service. He was interested and stopped to watch. Especially was his attention drawn to the leader of the group, the "bishop," who was Athanasius. He took a liking to the lad, and when he was old enough made him his secretary and then an archdeacon. Taking up the ascetic life Athanasius studied the classics and the Scriptures. In 325 he accompanied the bishop to the Council of Nicæa, where he made himself famous because of the stand he took against Arius. At the death of Alexander he became bishop, although against his protest. Five different times was he deposed and banished as a result of Arian controversies. Being a small man, but very quick of action, he was thought to have magic powers. He was greatly loved by his friends and greatly feared by his enemies. Yet he was one of the purest and most venerable personages of the Church. Gregory Nazianzen writes: "When I praise Athanasius, I praise virtue itself, because he combines all virtues in himself."

His one great object in life was to vindicate the deity of Christ. For this he spent most of his time, suffered deposition and twenty years of exile. Although he suffered persecution he did not practice it, but took the stand that orthodoxy should persuade faith and not force it.

Athanasius is distinguished for his theological depth and dialectic skill. Although his stormy career prevented him from writing long systematic works, he wrote much which was drawn from the circumstances at hand. Many of his books were hastily written while he was in temporary exile. His most important works are: *On the Incarnation of the Divine Word, On the Decrees of the Council of Nicæa, An Apology against the Arians, Commentary on the Psalms,* and *The Life of St. Anthony.*

BASIL, THE SHEPHERD OF SOULS

Basil was born at Cæsarea in 329 A.D. of a wealthy and pious family. His grandmother was St. Macrina and his mother St. Emmelia. His two brothers, Gregory of Nyssa and Peter of Sebaste, were bishops; and his sister, Macrina the Younger, was made a saint.

He received his early education from his father, who was a learned rhetorician. Later he studied at Constantinople and Athens. Here his two best friends were Gregory Nazianzen and the prince, Julian. Speaking of Athens, he says:

We knew only two streets of the city, the first and more excellent one to the churches and to the ministers of the altars; the other, which, however, we did not so highly esteem, to the public schools and to the teachers of the sciences. The streets to the theatres, games, and places of unholy amusement, we left to others.

After teaching rhetoric a few years in Cæsarea, he traveled in

Syria, Palestine, and Egypt, where he came into direct contact with the monastic life. It appealed to him so much that he sold all his property, gave the returns to the poor, and went to live in a little hut in a district of Pontus. Yet with all the beauties of nature about him—mountains, streams, broad plains—he was unable to flee from himself. He invited Gregory to live with him and together they had a wonderful time studying, praying, writing, and working at manual labor.

In 364 he was made a presbyter and in 370 was elected Bishop of Cæsarea, both elections being against his will. His great desire was to see peace within the Church. Wearing only one old garment, eating only bread, salt, and herbs, he labored faithfully among his people. Even the lepers were cared for in a hospital at Cæsarea by this noble shepherd of souls.

He was a great writer, using a pure, elegant, and vigorous style. Some of his works are: five books against Ennomnes, homilies on Creation, homilies on the Psalms, 365 epistles, and a work on the Holy Ghost.

GREGORY, THE THEOLOGIAN

Gregory Nazianzen was born in 330 A.D. in Cappodocia. His father was a bishop and his mother was Norma, one of the noblest women of the Christian Church. Having been well grounded in the Holy Scriptures and science through the training afforded by his parents, he continued his studies in Cæsarea, Alexandria, and Athens. In the latter place he formed a very close friendship with Basil.

After his studies were ended he adopted the ascetic life; but on a visit to his parents in 361, he was ordained presbyter by his father. This was done against his will; and on first impulse he fled from the city, but soon he returned and justified his actions. After the death of his father, in 374, he became bishop, but only for one year. In 375 he retired to his beloved solitude once more.

In 379 he was called to the pastoral charge at Constantinople. Here he did much to build up the faith and the Christian life of the people. Being a wonderful preacher, all classes came to hear his discourses on the vindication of the godhead of Christ.

With the exception of Chrysostom, he was the greatest orator of the Greek Church. After the victory at Nicæa, in which he played a very important part, he would have been appointed Bishop of Constantinople had not the Bishop of Egypt and of Macedonia objected on the ground that he still held the bishopric of Sasima. This wounded Gregory and he resigned his position. He died about 390. No records have been kept concerning the circumstances of his death.

We have two hundred and forty-two epistles by Gregory. They are very important, giving the history of the times, and in most cases are very interesting and well written. In his later life he wrote some poetry. Although it was never considered very great, it is valuable for the information it gives concerning his private life.

JOHN CHRYSOSTOM, THE GOLDEN-MOUTHED

John Chrysostom was born in 347 at Antioch. His father was a distinguished military officer and his mother, Anthusa, was a Christian woman of the highest type. She gave him a fine education, the germ of piety, and an understanding of the Bible. After receiving a literary training from Libanius, he became a rhetorician and a reader.

At the death of his mother he entered monastic solitude in the mountains near Antioch. Here he remained for six years under the direction of Diodonus. Although he enjoyed the life, his health broke down. He returned to Antioch in 380, where he was ordained a deacon and later made a presbyter. His sermons were of great power, so much so that they aroused the anger of Emperor Eudoxia and the envy of the patriarch Theophilus of Alexandria. Each sermon was carefully prepared through study of the Scriptures, prayer, and meditation. It was his custom to use whole books of the Bible, in place of different verses, for his texts. Often his sermons were interrupted by noisy demonstrations of applause. His message was one of strict discipline in Christian living, attacking boldly the vices of his age and the false, worldly, hypocritical religion of the court. He demanded that the people take Christianity in earnest, and used such noble, yet vigorous, fiery, and often overpowering language, that he led many into a higher way of living.

He opposed the Arians and was faithful to the Church doctrine, yet he avoided narrow dogmatism and angry controversy. Rather, he laid the emphasis on practical goodness and right living.

He ranks as the greatest of all pulpit orators, and was also great in homiletical exegesis. He wrote about six hundred homilies, and his *Pauline Epistles* are very highly esteemed. He also wrote a liturgy for the church service.

On September 14, 407, John Chrysostom died in banishment. His life had been one of persecution and undeserved suffering, which had but strengthened his character and heightened his fame. He was mourned by the Greeks and the Romans. His name is still celebrated among them.

AMBROSE, THE PRINCE OF THE CHURCH

Ambrose was born at Treves, Italy, in 340 A.D. Being the son of a governor of Gaul, he was educated at Rome for the highest civil offices. He distinguished himself as a rhetorician and was appointed imperial praetor of Upper Italy. In this position he enjoyed universal esteem.

After the death of Auxentius, Bishop of Milan, there was trouble over the election of his successor. They could arrive at no definite conclusion. Out of the confusion, a little child cried out, "Let Ambrose be bishop!"; and the people, judging it to be the voice of God, at once elected Ambrose bishop. At first he was terrified and tried to escape, but soon he submitted and in 374 was consecrated bishop. From that time on he lived entirely for the Church, becoming one of its greatest leaders. Not only did he live the ascetic life, but also the helpful life. Pure in his personal life, faithful to all his Church duties, always accessible to the poor and the needy, he was indeed a true prince.

The following example will show his great influence and power. Theodosius, the Emperor, had put many innocent people to death because of a riot at Thessalonica. Ambrose demanded repentance from him, meanwhile refusing him holy communion.

The Emperor refused many times, but finally submitted and made a public confession. Later he said that Ambrose was the only man who had ever dared to tell him the truth, and therefore became his true friend.

In 397 all Milan became greatly concerned because Ambrose was sick. They urged that he try to save himself. He replied: "I have so lived among you that I cannot be ashamed to live longer, but neither do I fear to die, for we have a good Lord."

Thus he died, mourned by both Jews and pagans, at the age of fifty-seven. Soon after his death many miracles were ascribed to him, which showed how much the people loved him.

His works are: *Exposition of Twenty-one Psalms, Commentary on the Gospel of Luke,* five books on faith, three on the Holy Ghost, and six on the sacraments. Also he wrote homilies, letters, music, and poetry. His liturgy is still used in the church at Milan.

JEROME, THE SCHOLAR

Jerome (340-419) was the most eloquent and interesting author of all the Latin fathers. He had a burning thirst for knowledge, a remarkable memory, a keen understanding, a quick and sound judgment, imagination, wit, and a brilliant power of expression. Being a student of Latin, Greek, and Hebrew, he collected a large and very valuable library of original works.

With all his learning he was not free from many of the faults of his age. Some say he lacked great depth of mind and character, that he had no strong convictions. Often he was vain, ambitious, and passionate. Realizing his wonderful intellectual ability, he became proud and gloried in his great knowledge. Many of his writings are full of envy, hatred, and anger, and contain many rhetorical exaggerations and unjust inferences.

But with all his faults, Jerome rendered lasting service to the world by translating the Bible into the Latin language. There was great need of such a work at this time, for there had been a decay of knowledge in the original languages of the Bible. Jerome, being a master of languages, was the only man fitted to undertake such a great task. The work began at Rome (382 to 385) at the suggestion of Pope Damasus and was not finished until twenty years later. Many charges were made against him by those who thought that he was a falsifier of the Scriptures and a disturber of the peace. But still he kept on, and soon the translation won approval on its own merits and became the clerical Bible of Western Christendom.

It deserves, as a whole, the highest praise for the boldness with which it went back from the half-deified Septuagint directly to the original Hebrew; for its union of fidelity and freedom; and the dignity, clearness, and gracefulness of its style.

—DANA CARLETON MUNRO

Other works of Jerome are his *Commentaries* or *Homilies*, his historical, doctrinal, and ethical writings, and his *Epistles*.

Augustine, the Christian Philosopher

Augustine was born November 13, 354, at Tagaste, North Africa. From his heathen father he inherited a love for the pleasures of the world, and from his Christian mother a deep yearning for God. He received his education at Madania, Carthage, Rome, and Milan. He accepted eagerly the carnal pleasures, mock wisdom, and skepticism of his age. It was only through the prayers of his mother, the sermons of Ambrose, and the Epistles of Paul that he was brought back to the Christian way.

His conversion took place in the garden of the Villa Cassiciacum, not far from Milan, in 386. Here he passed through many struggles of mind and heart until finally he "put on the Lord Jesus Christ." On Easter Sunday, 387, he was baptized by Ambrose at Milan. Selling all his goods for the poor, he broke with the world and lived a mildly ascetic life.

In 391 he was chosen presbyter of Hippo Requis. Later he became the bishop and for thirty-eight years made Hippo Requis the intellectual center of Western Christendom. By making his home a theological seminary, he began the Augustinian Order, which gave Martin Luther to the world.

As a philosophical and theological genius, he stands among

the first. His mind was "fertile and deep, bold and soaring, while his heart was full of love and humility." His writings abound in high ideals and sentiments, clear statements of truth, and strong arguments against error. Truly, he wrote from his heart to be understood by the people.

As a bishop he diligently ruled his church; as a preacher he surpassed all his contemporaries in practical usefulness. . . . We may deplore the extremes of his theology, but the whole world has gained from the example of his holiness and the outpourings of his religious genius.—FREDERIC W. FARRAR.

The most edifying works of Augustine are: *Confessions* (397) and *The City of God*. Also he wrote letters, apologetic works against pagans and Jews, and theological writings.

DOMINIC, THE FAITHFUL BUILDER

Dominic was born at Calaroga in 1170. Being a brilliant student he formed a close friendship with Diego of Acevedo, the Bishop of Osma. Together in 1203 they journeyed through southern France, where they found many Roman missionaries treated with contempt. Diego urged the missionaries to adopt a new system—one of self-denial, study, and apostolic poverty. In order to put his words into practice he formed a nunnery (1206), at Pronille, but he died in 1207 and Dominic took up the work. Many times Dominic was tempted to leave because of offers of bishoprics, but, taking Paul as his model, he remained steadfast. In 1215 he was presented with a house in Toulouse and, gathering likeminded men about him, he established an order which was recognized by Pope Honorius III in 1216. Dominic won men, as Paul had won them, by preaching. Using his home as a center he sent forth many missionaries to the great cities of learning, such as Paris, Rome, and Bologna. Through sacrifice and persecution and asceticism, these men carried the gospel to the people. But Dominic's order became less democratic as time went on. The high intellectualism of the order gave it quite an aristocratic flavor, thus causing it to lose much of its influence. Dominic died in 1221.

FRANCIS OF ASSISI, THE IMITATOR OF CHRIST

Giovanni Bernadore (Francis of Assisi) was born in 1181 or 1182, at Assisi, in central Italy. He soon acquired the nickname of Francisco (Francis), which in time supplanted his real name. His father was a cloth merchant and was quite disappointed by the reckless ways of his son. For a time Francis was held as a prisoner of war in Perugia. Then he was taken with a very serious sickness, which, more than anything else, helped to bring out the deeper side of his life.

His conversion was gradual. In the first place, his heart was touched by the suffering of some lepers. Then, while on a pilgrimage to Rome, he heard a divine command to restore the fallen house of God. Taking this command literally he sold a large amount of his father's cloth and rebuilt the ruined church of St. Damian, near Assisi. As a result of this episode his disgusted father disinherited him in 1206.

For the next two years, Francis went about aiding and restoring churches, preaching the gospel of repentance. He lived in the simplest manner, taking the words of Matthew 10: 7-14 in a literal sense. It was his purpose to imitate Christ and obey his commands in a most realistic way. He said that, "the most High revealed to me that I ought to live according to the model of the Holy Gospel."

Soon he had gathered about him many likeminded associates who also were imitators of Christ. They were bound together by love and practiced the utmost poverty, for they believed that only in this way could the world be fully redeemed and Christ really followed. They were at first called "Brethren." They represented such a fine type of character that Pope Innocent III gave his approval to their organization.

Francis was not much of an organizer and, as the order grew very rapidly, the former rules became inadequate. A new rule was adopted by Cardinal Ugolim of Ostea which included: prescribed obedience to the order's officers, established fixed costumes, and irrevocable vows. In fact the whole tone of the order was changed so much that Francis was grieved and withdrew from the world.

On October 3, 1226 he died in the church of Portimmenla bearing on his body what many believed to be the reproduction of Christ's wounds. Two years later he was made a saint by Pope Gregory IX, and few men have deserved the title more.

He was patient and humble, yet he "possessed an original and well-balanced mind, extraordinary common sense, an iron will, and indomitable courage." . . . Of all the medieval saints he was probably the one who would seem least out of place in the twentieth century.—DANA CARLETON MUNRO.

BERNARD, THE TRUE SAINT

Bernard (1090 to 1153) was born of knightly ancestry in Fontaines. With thirty companions he entered a monastery at Citeana where he remained three years and then went to Clairvaux, where he established a monastery. Here he remained the rest of his life as its abbot.

"Above all, men admired in Bernard a moral force, a consistency of character, which added weight to all that he said and did." These words of Munro tell us why Bernard was the greatest man of his age. Munro goes on to say:

His absolute faith and intense love of asceticism made of him a perfect monk; his eloquence, piety, and ability caused him to become the arbiter between kings and rival popes. His keen knowledge of affairs, excellent judgment and executive ability caused his aid to be sought on every important occasion; he responded to every call and gave his services wherever they were needed because he felt it to be a duty; but he longed passionately to return to his cell apart from the world.

On the whole Bernard did not care a great deal for study or unnecessary knowledge. Once, in a sermon before a group of students, he cried, "Flee from Babylon and save your souls"; and, as a result, twenty of the students became monks. His complex character is very hard to understand, but his life showed that he was a man of lovable character and of commanding ability, standing among the world's great men.

Here is a short list of some of the things he did: founded the monastery of Clairvaux; broke the papal schism by electing

Innocent to the office of pope; reconciled the Emperor Lothian with the Hohenstaufens; established peace between Genoa and Pisa; secured recognition for the Knights Templars; preached the second Crusade; persuaded Conrad, Emperor of Germany, to take the Cross; and established peace at Metz, where nobles and citizens were in murderous combat.

He died in 1153, the best known and most widely mourned man of his time.

> "Yes, write it in the rock," Saint Bernard said,
> "Grave it on brass with adamantine pen!
> 'Tis God Himself becomes apparent, when
> God's wisdom and God's goodness are display'd."
>
> LONGFELLOW

HELPS FOR STUDY

Written Work

1. What type of man was Eusebius? What was his most important work?

2. Give a brief outline of the life of Athanasius.

3. Why is Basil called "The Shepherd of Souls." What kind of a life did he live?

4. What great ability or abilities did Gregory have?

5. What is Chrysostom noted for?

6. What incident caused Ambrose to become bishop of Milan? Was he a success?

7. What great service did Jerome render to the world?

8. Why is Augustine called the "Christian Philosopher"?

9. Where did Dominic spend most of his life and do most of his work?

10. In what way did Francis of Assisi imitate Christ?

11. What did Bernard do for his age?

Oral Discussion

1. Of what value is the study of biography?

2. How is Christian character made?

3. Should the modern Church do more to influence the course of history?

4. Is there such a thing as a "self-made man"?

5. What part does environment play in the development of character?

6. How have the various denominations united to provide relief and reconstruction aid?

Special Assignments

1. Collect ten quotations which deal with great men in history.

2. List some of the qualities which make for character.

3. Write a paper on "The Successful Life."

4. Show that hymns prove the lack of change in real Christianity throughout the ages.

5. Study the life of Boniface, Apostle of Germany.

6. Study the life of Alfred the Great, King of England.

7. Discover something about the following men: Hildebrand, Thomas Aquinas, Thomas à Becket, Thomas à Kempis.

12

THE GREAT DIVIDE
1054 A.D.

Then welcome each rebuff
That turns earth's smoothness rough,
Each sting that bids nor sit nor stand but go!
Be our joys three-parts pain!
Strive, and hold cheap the strain;
Learn, nor account the pang; dare, never grudge the throe!

BROWNING

Causes Leading Up to the Divide

Principal Adeney of Lancashire College says:

The most momentous fact in the history of Christendom during the Middle Ages is the separation between the Eastern and the Western Churches.

In order fully to appreciate this statement, it is necessary to note the characteristics of these two bodies.

At first we notice their great likenesses. In doctrine, ritual, and discipline they are very much alike. Both accept the Nicene Creed and are sacramental and episcopal. Their chief difference lies in the emphasis put on these special beliefs and practices. The Eastern Church stressed orthodoxy and became known as "The Holy Orthodox Church," while the Western Church stressed catholicity and was called "The Roman Catholic Church."

It was as a result of centuries of misunderstanding that the division finally took place. The East and the West were of different races and languages, having mental and moral differences.

87

The East was Greek in blood, used the Greek language in its worship and its theology; while the West was Latin, using the Latin language in the ritual of the Church. This difference in race and language played a large rôle in the final separation.

The next logical step was the division of the Eastern and Western Empires. When Constantine transferred the capital from the Tiber to the shores of the Bosphorus, he also moved with it the center of social and intellectual influence. This left the West unaided, and when the Gothic hosts came down upon it, instead of turning to the East for help, it turned to the Franks. On Christmas day, 800 A.D., the pope crowned Charles the Great as Emperor, thus definitely breaking all political relationships with the East.

Another cause for this separation resulted from the conflict between the pope at Rome and the patriarch at Constantinople. The situation became acute when Ignatius, in 857, refused to administer the sacrament to Cæsar Bardas because of his immorality. Ignatius was tried, and on a false accusation of sedition, was imprisoned. Photius, a highly educated man, took his place. From the very first he began to look down upon the pope who was his inferior both in learning and in brain power. At a council held at St. Sophia, Photius reaffirmed the Nicene Creed, but without the *Filioque* clause which the Latin had added. As a result of this action the pope pronounced an anathema on Photius. Now it only needed the final step to make the division of the Western and Eastern churches complete.

JUST A WORD

Barrie tells us, in his *Sentimental Tommy*, how Tommy brought scorn upon himself by the lack of a word. This happened in the case of the Eastern Church. Only one word, yet what great harm it wrought! It broke a great universal Church into two parts and separated them as far as the East is from the West. One would think it hardly possible that the chief difference in doctrine held by these two bodies could be so small as to rest upon one word. But that was the case.

According to Adeney: "The last stage of the long quarrel was concerned with the controversy on the *Filioque* clause of the Nicene Creed." That is, the Greek Church maintained that the Holy Spirit proceeds from the Son, while the Latin Church maintained that the Holy Spirit comes from the Son as a joint source with the Father. In order to adjust the Nicene Creed to their doctrine, the Latin Church added the word *Filioque* to the creed, making it read *"qui a Patre Filioque procedit,"* instead of *"qui a Patre procedit."* This led the Greek Church to accuse the Latin Church of sin, because of the fact that they changed the venerated Nicene Creed. And so, even to this present day, the two churches stand divided on this point and without any hope of reconciliation, for each body has anathematized the other for its action.

THE FINAL BLOW

In 1053 A.D., Michael Cerularius, Patriarch of Constantinople, sent a letter to the bishops of Apulia in which he expressed the desire for closer union between the East and the West. He also included in the letter a statement of the chief differences of doctrine and practice held by the two churches, which included the Dogma of the Procession from the Son and the use of un-leavened bread at the Eucharist (practised by the West alone). The letter fell into the hands of Pope Leo IX who addressed a reply to the patriarch which was intended to make him submit to the pope and adopt the Latin ritual. This the patriarch refused to do and on July 16, 1054, the papal legates placed on the altar of St. Sophia a sentence of anathema upon Michael and his supporters. "Let them Anathema Maranatha, with Simoniacs, Valehians, Donatist, Nicholaitans, Leverians, Pneumatomchi, Manichus, and Nazarenes and with all heretics: yea, with the devil and his angels: Amen, Amen, Amen."

THE CHURCH OF THE EAST GOES ITS OWN WAY

It is hard for the West to understand the Eastern Church, for it has its own traditions and its own peculiar spirit and character. It can be called neither Protestant nor Roman Catholic, since it broke with the latter and had no connection with the Protestant Reformation. It has, however, much in common with evangelical Protestantism both in spirit and practice.

This Church truly knows the meaning of the words "persecution," "struggle," "endurance," and "martyrdom." It has experienced them all and has developed a religion of mystery as a result of much meditation upon the things of the spirit. In speaking of their worship, Frank Gavin says,

"In the details of Eastern worship is a rough epitome of the history of Eastern Christendom: the *ikons*, about which a bitter controversy was once waged; the service in the vernacular as against Latin; the existence of both a married and a celibate priesthood; the strong and passionate loyalty to the national allegiance evidenced by the provision of special prayers for the rulers by name—all these mark the characteristics, peculiarities, and contrasts with the customs of the West."

The Eastern Church has been retarded in its development because it has been struggling for centuries against the invasions of Arabic and Turkish Mohammedans. Nevertheless, it made a tremendous advance during the period of the nineteenth century. New schools and seminaries were built, the clergy became highly educated, and many theologians and writers of note were developed. This Church with its millions of Christians has taken on a new lease of life, and is expected to make a great contribution to the new interpretation of the Christian way of living for tomorrow. Certain sections of it are now officially members of the World Council of Churches.

HELPS FOR STUDY

Written Work

1. Give the causes which led up to the division of the Eastern and the Western churches.

2. Explain what is meant by the "*Filioque* clause."

3. What caused the final separation of the two Christian bodies?

4. What has been the nature of the Eastern Church since the separation?

Oral Discussion

1. What influence has communism had on the Russian Orthodox Church?

2. Why does not the World Council of Churches include the whole of Christendom?

3. What harm results from misunderstanding?

4. Was Jesus really the Son of God, or was he merely a man who came the nearest to becoming like God?

5. In what way does Jesus separate his followers from the world?

Special Assignments

1. Write a short paper on the contribution of the Eastern spirit of meditation to religion.

2. Make a study of the present religious conditions in the Eastern Church.

3. Discuss the debt which we owe to the Eastern Church.

4. Find out what is happening today between Islam and other religions.

13

FIGHTING FOR THE CHURCH
1096-1254 A.D.

Francis Greenwood Peabody, in *The Church of the Spirit* says:

To put on the whole armor of God, to enlist in the cause of Christ with soldierly obedience—this call to service has been through all the Christian centuries the inspiration of missionary effort, the challenge to heroism, and the prophecy of victory. No hymn stirs a Christian gathering to more vigorous participation than the martial summons: "Onward, Christian Soldiers! Marching as to war." The thought of a mighty army on its march to conquest is an exhilarating, even if it be at times an ironical appeal to a peaceful and comfortable congregation.

And so it is with the crusaders of the Middle Ages. The thought of their going forth to fight for Christ gives one both a thrill and a sense of misdirected zeal.

BACK OF THE SCENES

The eleventh and twelfth centuries were great revolutionary ages. Out of the darkness and disorder of the old grew a better and more advanced age. Europe at this period first began to have a soul and felt, as never before, that it was part of a great world system.

During 970 to 1040 A.D., forty-eight famines occurred in Europe. Thousands of people died on every hand. The overpopulation was tremendous and, since there were no means of remedying the situation, life was not worth living for most of the common people. If it had not been for the Church civilization would have been lost altogether. Christianity gave to the world a hope. Many entered the monastic and ascetic life. Great value came to be placed upon relics and pilgrimages; so much so that from every country of Europe many hundreds of wanderers made their way to the Holy Land each year. Religion was their first great concern in life.

As home life was not very pleasant, a spirit of adventure began to develop in order that wealth and glory might be gained. Out of this grew the great system of knight-errantry which played so large a part in the crusades. The knights loved nothing better than to fight for a cause, and especially against the heathen.

As a result of these three influences—the Church, the ascetic idea of life, and the love of military exploits—a foundation was built upon which one of the most thrilling dramas of history was staged.

THE GREATEST SPEECH IN HISTORY

The Turks had captured Jerusalem and all Asia Minor was in their hands. The Emperor Alexius, wishing to regain this territory, called upon Pope Urban II for aid, and so, at the Council of Clermont (1095), Urban II appealed to the Christians to save the Holy Land. So great were the results of this eloquent speech that it is called the greatest speech in history. In order that the power of the speech may be appreciated, two sections of it are given here.

We have heard, most beloved brethren, and you have heard what we cannot recount without deep sorrow—how, with great hurt and dire sufferings, our Christian brothers, members in Christ, are scourged, oppressed, and injured in Jerusalem, in Antioch, and other cities of the East. Your own blood-brothers, your companions, your associates (for you are sons of the same Christ and the same church) are either subjected in their inherited homes to their masters, or are driven from them, or they come as beggars among us; or, which is far worse, they are flogged, and exiled as slaves for sale in their own land. Christian blood, redeemed by the blood of

Christ, has been shed, and Christian flesh, akin to the flesh of Christ, has been subjected to unspeakable degradation, and servitude. . . . Holy men do not possess these cities; nay, base and bastard Turks hold sway over our brothers. . . .

In these temperate regions you were born and you have therefore a title to victory which your enemies can never acquire. You have prudence, you have discipline, you have skill and valour, and you will go forth, through the gift of God and the privilege of St. Peter, absolved from all your sins. The consciousness of this freedom shall soothe the toil of your journey, and death will bring to you the benefits of a blessed martyrdom. Sufferings and torments may perhaps await you. You may picture them to yourselves as the most exquisite tortures, and the picture may perhaps fall short of the agony which you may have to undergo; but your sufferings will redeem your souls at the expense of your bodies. Go then, on your errand of love, of love for the faithful who in the lands overcome by the infidel cannot defend themselves; of love which will put out of sight all the ties that bind you to the spots which you have called your homes. Your homes, in truth, they are not. For the Christian all the world is exile, and all the world is at the same time his country. If you leave a rich patrimony here, a better patrimony is promised you in the Holy Land. They who die will enter the mansions of heaven, while the living shall behold the sepulchre of their Lord. Blessed are they who, taking this vow upon them, shall inherit such a recompense: happy they who are led to such a conflict, that they may share in such rewards.

The people cried out with one voice: "It is the will of God! It is the will of God!"

The pope went on:

It is, in truth, his will! and let these words be your war-cry when you unsheath your swords against the enemy. You are soldiers of the cross: wear, then, on your breast or on your shoulders the blood-red sign of him who died for the salvation of your souls. Wear it as a token that his help will never fail you: wear it as the pledge of a vow which can never be recalled.

THE PEOPLE'S CRUSADE, 1096 TO 1099

The hearts of the people of the West had been touched. Unable to wait for leadership, many groups set out for the Holy Land. Two groups or, more exactly two leaderless mobs, thinking that the Hungarians must be infidels, committed such excesses that they in turn were all massacred. Another mob persecuted the Jews in Germany and were likewise massacred. Others reached Constantinople, but were so disorderly that they were sent into Asia Minor where they were slaughtered by the Turks.

In 1096 three great armies were organized. They were composed of nobles and knights from France, Normandy, Flanders, England, Italy, and Sicily. While there were only about 100,000 real fighters, counting the monks, women and children, and camp followers, there were some hundreds of thousands. Meeting at Nicæa they marched through the Cilician Gates to Antioch and after almost a year's siege took the city. Many of the Crusaders remained here, but Godfrey of Bouillon went on with the rest to Jerusalem. After a month's siege the city was taken and the slaughter which followed was terrible (July 15, 1099).

Daimbert, Archbishop of Pisa, in his official summary of the Crusades, tells the story in this way:

Accordingly, with God as our Fellow-Voyager and Helper, we came even to Jerusalem. And while the army was laboring in the siege of that city with great difficulty, especially on account of the scarcity of water, a council was held, and the bishops and princes announced that a procession was to be made around the city with bare feet. [This was done] that He who had entered it in humility for our sake, might, through our humility, open it to us to do justice on His enemies for His sake. Accordingly, the Lord, pleased at this humility, granted the city with His enemies to us on the eighth day after our humiliation. . . . And, if you desire to know what was done about the enemy whom we found there, know that in the portico of Solomon and in his Temple, our men rode in the blood of the Saracens up to the knees of the horses.

Thus ended the First Crusade—in human blood.

THE MONKS' CRUSADE (1147 TO 1149)

It was through the preaching of St. Bernard that the Second

Crusade was made possible. With an influence second to no other man of his age, with such eloquence that would even stir the most peaceful to action, he repeated the scenes which had taken place at Clermont as a result of the appeal of Pope Urban II. He sent forth the Knights Templars with this message of death ringing in their ears:

> The Christian who slays the unbeliever in the Holy Land is sure of his reward, more sure if he is slain. The Christian glories in the death of the Pagan, because by it Christ is glorified; by his own death both he himself and Christ are still more glorified.

The reason of this crusade was the capture of Edessa by the Turks. Although, as just seen, St. Bernard aroused a great deal of enthusiasm, this crusade was far less successful than the first. Both Emperor Conrad III and King Louis of France participated in this crusade, each having the following of a large army. But because of the treachery of Emperor Manuel of Constantinople and that of the bribed barons at Palestine, because of the lack of interest of the Franks in the cause who were then enjoying the life in Palestine, and because of the sins committed by the army, the Second Crusade ended in utter shame. All the prophecies of St. Bernard had failed, and he was bitterly attacked by the people. Pointing out that the failure was the result of the immoral life of the pilgrims and the treachery of supposed friends, he finally freed himself from guilt. The Second Crusade left the people with a cry of anguish in their hearts.

THE KINGS' CRUSADE (1189 TO 1192)

Saladin, ruler of Egypt, preached to the Moslems a counter-crusade, a Holy War—fighting against the Christians. Thus it became a matter of crusader against crusader, religion against religion, Islam against Christianity. In 1187 Jerusalem was captured by the Moslems. This began the Third Crusade in 1189. It was a grand affair. Chivalry and romance, plunder and greed, took the place of the religious motive. The crusade was led by three kings: Frederick Barbarossa of Germany, Philip Augustus of France, and Richard the Lion-hearted of England. Frederick died before he reached the Holy Land, and his army was broken up. Philip and Richard had a disgraceful quarrel at Acre, and Philip returned to France with his army. After capturing Acre and leaving several hundred thousand infidels slaughtered in cold blood, Richard moved on to capture Azotus, Jaffa, and Ascalon. Reaching Bethlehem, he found that he had insufficient troops to conquer Jerusalem. Returning to Acre, he fought a battle with Saladin and was victorious. A truce was formed, giving the Christians possession of the coast shore of Palestine and free access into Jerusalem. Thus ended the Third Crusade, with Jerusalem still in the control of the "infidels."

THE KNIGHTS' CRUSADE (1202 TO 1204)

The failure of the enterprises in the Holy Land greatly afflicted the soul of the new pope, Innocent III. As a result of his efforts thousands of knights and nobles of France set out for Palestine. They engaged the Venetians to build ships, but upon arrival at Venice were not able to pay for them. To get sufficient funds, they plundered the Christian city of Zara. Then they marched on to Constantinople, captured and sacked it, establishing the Latin Empire of Constantinople which lasted for fifty-seven years. This conduct was indefensible and criminal, leading to the downfall of the city at the hands of the Turks in 1453. Thus ended the Fourth Crusade, not even having reached the Holy Land.

THE CHILDREN'S CRUSADE (1212)

Here is one of the saddest episodes in all history. The stories of the adventures and excitement of the crusaders had fired the hearts of the boys and girls of Europe. It took only the appeal of unwise preachers to start them off for Jerusalem. Thinking that supernatural power would be given them, the young Davids and Judiths set forth. One lad, named Nicholas, led a great company as far as the Alps, where many starved to death. Other groups were seized by Saracen kidnapers, who took them as slaves for Eastern fields or harems. Of the seven vessels which were loaded with Christian children at Marseilles five reached

Egypt consigned to slave markets; and two were wrecked off the isle of St. Peter, where Pope Gregory IX afterward caused a church to be built in memory of the victims. Thus ended this Crusade—a "slaughter of the innocents."

THE POPE'S CRUSADE (1228 TO 1229)

Pope Innocent III used this tragedy as the basis for another crusade. "These children," he said, "reproach us with being asleep while they were flying to the assistance of the Holy Land." All Europe received a special appeal from the Pope to furnish the necessary men, ships, and money to support this crusade; as a result, the largest force of all the crusades was raised. At the head of the group was the Patriarch of Jerusalem. The army reached the Holy Land safely but was unable to capture Jerusalem. The crusade was saved from utter failure by the arrival of fresh troops from Germany, who were "led by a cross in the sky and had squadrons of angels fighting for them." Leaving Palestine, they departed for Egypt. They were very successful and were offered terms of peace three different times, which would have given them all of the Holy Land. But Cardinal Pelagius refused each time. These refusals exhausted the patience of the Sultan, and he caused all the canals of lower Egypt to be flooded. The Christian camps "were thus caught in the midst of the waters like fish in a net." The haughty cardinal now begged for peace. Brave King John of Brienne then fell down at the feet of the Sultan and burst into tears because his people were perishing in the waters. The Sultan, respecting his courage, immediately provisioned the Christian camp and, to the Christians' great shame, sent his own son to lead them out of the land which they had come to conquer. Thus ended the Fifth Crusade, with a Turk acting as a Good Samaritan.

RESULTS OF THE CRUSADES

There were four other crusades, but they were of no very great importance. Even when we consider the first five crusades, in respect to their purpose, they were all failures. The Holy Land remained unconquered, the advancing Mohammedans were not retarded, and the cost in lives and money had been enormous. Nevertheless, in an indirect way, the crusades did a great deal of good. They brought about the turning point in the Middle Ages. Commerce and trade routes were established; a new political element—the town—came into being; also, an intellectual awakening, theological, artistic, and architectural advancement, took place. On these a foundation for the Reformation—the transition into modern history—was laid. From this time on history grows more and more diversified, breaking forth in the form of many nations and creative activities.

Let us remember, as we leave this story of the bloody champions of Christianity, these few lines of Thomas Moore:

> The sword may pierce the beaver,
> Stone walls in time may sever,
>   'Tis mind alone,
>   Worth steel and stone,
> That keep men free forever.

HELPS FOR STUDY

Written Work

1. What three influences laid the foundation for the crusades?
2. Why is the speech of Urban II said to be the greatest in history?
3. Give an outline of the First Crusade.
4. What caused the failure of the Second Crusade?
5. Why did the Third Crusade result in a failure?
6. What happened to the Fourth Crusade?
7. Give an account of the Children's Crusade.
8. What caused the failure of the Fifth Crusade?
9. Give both the bad and the good results of the crusades.

Oral Discussion

1. Did Christ ever ask anyone to fight for him?
2. What attitude should a Christian take in regard to peacetime compulsory military training?
3. Can the crusaders be justified?

4. Were not the Moslems fighting just as "holy" a war as the Christians?

5. To what degree has the foreign-mission enterprise become a modern crusade?

6. How can we establish a just and lasting peace?

Special Assignments

1. List the different motives appealed to in Urban's speech.

2. Write a paper on the cruelty of the crusaders.

3. Discuss the psychology of the crusades.

4. Discover what effects the capture of Constantinople by the Turks had on world progress.

5. Read or see a play based upon the life of Joan of Arc.

6. Look up something about Frederick Barbarossa.

·14·

THE DECAY OF POWER
. . . the Decline of the Papacy

All things decay with time; the forest sees
The growth and downfall of her aged trees:
That timber tall, which threescore lustres stood
The proud dictator of the state-like wood—
I mean the sovereign of all plants, the oak,
Droops, dies, and falls, without the cleaver's stroke.

HERRICK

THE "BABYLONIAN CAPTIVITY"

The zenith of power and glory of the Roman Catholic Church has been reached. Now comes its decline and decay. In 1305 the cardinals elected a Frenchman as head of the Church. Instead of going to Rome he remained in France and set up a papal court at Avignon on the lower Rhone. Here the popes remained for seventy years, becoming in a very true sense vassals of the French kings who used them as tools with which to gain their selfish ends. Conditions became so disgraceful that historians have called this period the "Babylonian Captivity" of the papacy, insomuch as it resembled the captivity of the Jews in Babylonia.

One of the worst crimes in history—the destruction of the Knights Templars—was the joint work of these popes and the French king. This order had become very wealthy and the king and the nobility owed them vast sums of money. With charges of "heresy" the pope and king began their attack. Criminal investigations, torture and burning at the stake were the orders

101

of the day, and in 1312 the Templars were suppressed. Their great wealth passed into the hands of the king and nobles, and what was left went to the Hospitalers, a rival order.

THREE IN ONE

It happened that one of these popes from Avignon died while making a visit in Rome. Immediately, hoping to bring the head of the Church back to Rome once more, the cardinals elected an Italian as pope (1378). But a few months later they realized the great mistake that they had made. Urban VI, the new pope, was a rough old man with a very fiery temper and would listen to no counsel save his own—and that was exceedingly warped. In disgust the cardinals fled to Avignon, declared their former election null and void, since they had been forced into a hasty decision, elected a new pope, Clement VII, a Frenchman, who made his headquarters at Avignon. But Urban VI still maintained that he was pope, having been elected by the cardinals and therefore, in truth, the infallible mediator between God and man, the head of the Church, the vicar of Christ, the possessor of the keys. Clement VII claimed the same power. Thus behold how great a marvel! Two popes, both elected by the same cardinals, both claiming the some power, both the head of the same Church, each denouncing the other as the emissary of Satan himself! Thus for a time there were two great Churches in Europe, resulting in what is called the "Great Schism of the West" and the "Balance of Power." France, Scotland, and Spain supported the pope at Avignon. England, Germany, and Italy supported the pope at Rome.

Finally, in 1409, at the Council of Pisa, both of the popes were deposed by the cardinals, and they elected Alexander II as the new pope. But the two other popes refused to recognize the action taken by the council, each being unwilling to forfeit his power. Thus we have a still more glorious spectacle —three popes—each having a considerable following!

In 1414 the Council of Constance was called. Through deposition, death, and the use of force, all of the anti-popes were put out of the way, and the unity of the Church was finally established by the election of Martin V as pope. Thus the schism ended, never to occur again in the Roman Catholic Church.

ATTEMPTS AT REFORM

As a result of these anti-popes, cries for reform came from every side. Church taxes were extremely high. Christianity was losing its simplicity; its leaders were living in luxury while the mass of people starved. Councils for reform were held; first the Council of Pisa (1409) and then the Council of Constance (1414 to 1418). But the first Council failed utterly to reform the Church. The Council of Constance was more successful. It was a brilliant affair, being headed by the Emperor Sigismund and Pope John XXIII, with cardinals and the laity of many nations taking part. It was the first great international congress of Europe and was held at Constance, a city of eight thousand people, easily accessible to the nations north of the Alps. It is said that the total number of strangers who gathered at the Council ranged from 50,000 to 100,000. It took two thousand "special constables" to maintain order and, in spite of them, five thousand people were drowned in a lake.

One of the chief difficulties with the conference was the lack of money. Sigismund, who was the chairman, borrowed great sums of money from the German princes. One of these princes was Frederic of Hohenzollern, who was rewarded for his kindness by the gift of the Duchy of Brandenburg, which later became the Kingdom of Prussia. The aims of the Council were: "to restore unity, to reform the Church in head and members, and to purge the Church of erroneous doctrines." We just noted how the first aim was carried out—a new pope was elected. The second aim was laid aside while the third was being carried out. John Huss was condemned and burned. The writings of Wycliffe were destroyed; and his bones, which rested in Lutterworth, were burned and thrown into the River Swift. The second aim was complicated because of national rivalries and its vagueness. Many wanted to get home, for, sad to say, England took advantage of the Council and invaded France, fighting the battle of Agincourt while the Council was in session. After many useless debates, it was decided to have such councils every eight years to take care of such matters as reforms. Otherwise, nothing about reforming was done. The first of these succeeding councils met at Basel (1431 to 1449), but it only resulted in a conflict between the papal and anti-papal powers.

Although these three councils did not accomplish much in the way of reform, they made the people realize that reform could never come within the hierarchy itself. It was coming, not through resolution, but through revolution.

Lost Zeal

Missionary effort during this period ceased. The causes were many and varied in their nature. All Europe was now inside the Church. The East could not be penetrated because of the barrier set up by the Greek Catholic Church and the Mohammedans. The New World had not been discovered. As a result there was a condition of stagnation and decline in the Church. Spiritual life was lacking. There was no real desire for missionary activity. The religion of Jesus was lost in the multitude of creeds and ceremonies. In short, the spiritual motivation of Christ was missing.

Bernard Lord Manning gives a fine summary of the reasons for this lack of zeal in the following words:

The Middle Ages seem to be a period of great ideas, imperfectly carried out: the idea of a Christian Church united under the supreme pontiff; of a Christian world ruled by the representative of the ancient Roman Empire; of an organized system by which the rich protected the poor; of property based on the discharge of its obligations; of chivalry and romance; of industry combined in the brotherhood of guilds; above all an idea of society based on Christian principles. These failed not because the ideas were not noble, but that they were ignobly perverted. Sometimes they worked well for a time and became later obsolete or corrupted by man's selfishness. A single State guided by a united Church promotes peace but encourages less freedom. Feudalism, designed as a remedy for anarchy and to give every man in an elaborately graded society his rights, ended by being organized oppression. The romance of chivalry lingered till the professional soldier took the place of the knight going forth in quest of adventures in honor of his lady. Guilds degenerated into selfish combinations to restrict trade, while Christian idealism gave way before the growing materialism of the age of the Renaissance.

> We have but faith: we cannot know;
> For knowledge is of things we see;
> And yet we trust it comes from Thee.
> A beam in darkness; let it grow.
>
> **TENNYSON**

HELPS FOR STUDY

Written Work

1. What is meant by the "Babylonian captivity"?
2. Explain how there happened to be three popes at the same time.
3. What attempts were made to reform the Church?
4. Why did missionary activity cease?

Oral Discussion

1. What is the test of real success?
2. How could three popes each be infallible?
3. What are some of the arguments for and against Church union?
4. Can sin ever be entirely wiped out of a life?
5. Is the Roman Catholic Church today stronger than ever before in its history?
6. Which is the most important in religion, the heart or the mind?

Special Assignments

1. With the help of the *Canterbury Tales* (about 1384), give Chaucer's attitude in regard to the Church.
2. What attitude does Langland take? (See *Piers Plowman.*)
3. Compare the *Koran* with our *Bible*.
4. Write a paper on "The Architecture of the Middle Ages."
5. Make a list of the great artists of the Renaissance.

· 15 ·

THE CHURCH AWAKES
. . . the Reformation in Europe
1517-1648

I am afraid that a great revolution is pending.—ERASMUS

DREAMS OF BETTER THINGS

Between the councils for reform and the Reformation is a period called the Renaissance—a time when nations began to realize that they were alive and that life was really worth living. Browning's lines express the new attitude: "How good is man's life, the mere living! How fit to employ all the heart and the soul and the senses forever in joy!"

The change was from "other-wordliness" to "worldliness," used in the best sense of the term. The discovery of America, the return to classical scholarship, the paintings of Raphael, the plays of Shakespeare, the discovery that the world revolves about the sun, the printing of books, and other events were not the greatest things which happened during this period. Greater than all these were revival of the human mind and spirit, the realization of man's possibilities, the awakening to the beauties of this world, and the appreciation of the joys in this present life.

The Renaissance had a vital effect upon the Roman Church. Some of the popes became converted to the new spirit and beautified Rome with Renaissance architecture, built vast libraries, employed Raphael and Michelangelo to decorate their churches, and built the wonderful St. Peter's by selling indulgences. Many of the priests caught the new spirit of art and learning and were soon to rebel against the old systems of the Church which were being outgrown. In fact, the spirit of the Renaissance entered the minds of all the leaders of Europe and in the end really turned the thinking of the world upside down.

In Germany the Renaissance resulted in a movement called "Humanism." It was led by Erasmus, "the citizen of Europe." He believed that they had buried the chief virtues—love, humility, purity—under the heavy pile of doctrine and ceremony. He wanted people to be reasonable, to use their common sense; he maintained that the doctrines taught in the monasteries, churches, and schools were not sensible. His "Praise of Folly" was a satire written to show the absurdity of man-made Christianity with all its illogical beliefs, such as the miraculous power of images of the saints, the purchasing of indulgences to escape the torments of purgatory, and the like. Besides this critical way of transforming Christian thought, he used the constructive method—that of recalling men to primitive Christianity. He translated volume after volume of the Church fathers and wrote a new Latin translation of the New Testament, making many improvements over the Vulgate. He had little faith in the methods used by the Protestant party, for he believed that a transformation would come quite naturally as a result of the new intellectual spirit of the Renaissance. A contemporary wrote, "The jokes of Erasmus did the Pope more harm than the anger of Luther," which shows his great influence upon the mind of the people during this period. Erasmus, in a very true sense, prepared the way for the great reformer, Martin Luther.

THE PROTESTANT, MARTIN LUTHER

Martin Luther was born November 10, 1483, in Eisleben, Germany. His parents were simple people, with a good amount of piety, and they gave him the best schooling that Germany could afford. He had a brilliant record as a student and planned, upon his graduation from the University of Erfurt, to practice law. But his plans were destroyed by the sudden death of a friend and by a narrow escape from death which caused him such anxiety for his soul's salvation that he entered a monastery of Augustinian hermits in Erfurt, July, 1505. He was such a scholarly monk that he soon gained wide recognition. In 1512 he became a lecturer on the Bible and the district vicar of eleven monasteries. Later he became professor in the University of Wittenberg.

In 1512 he was sent to Rome on business by the Augustinian order and was startled by the loose living and lifeless religion which he found there. On his return he applied himself to the study of the Bible and began teaching justification by faith, as found in the "Epistle to the Romans" and "the Epistle to the Galatians." When Johann Tetzel, a Dominican monk, came into his district selling indulgences, that the great St. Peter's might be built, Luther rose up in rebellion and nailed "ninety-five theses" on the castle church at Wittenberg (October, 1517), attacking indulgences, both in practice and in theory. But it was not his purpose to have the practice abandoned altogether, only to restore it to its former position. The theses were merely intended for academic debate. Instead, they stirred up the people of the whole nation and, in the end, changed the entire course of the Christian Church. Luther then became the center of a mighty upheaval of religious thought, which soon got beyond his control and pushed forward in wild confusion over all Europe. As a result Luther was summoned to Rome, but taking the advice of the Elector of Saxony he refused to go. In 1520 he was excommunicated by the Church and in 1521 he was placed under the ban of the Empire by the Diet of Worms. During the time which he was under this ban he worked on a translation of the Bible. The work was finished in 1534. He gave the German people a translation of the Scriptures which was idiomatic and very readable, insomuch that it largely determined the form of speech of future German literature. In all the history of translation there is no achievement that can equal this. It was the first translation to be made directly from the Greek text into ordinary, everyday language.

Luther is therefore the great hero of the Protestant world.

He gave to men a new sense of religious freedom and a radiant faith in God. He was a prophet in the midst of mighty nations, voicing a spirit of adventurous Christianity and self-determination in religion. There have been very few men who have influenced the course of history as much as Martin Luther. When he finished his work in 1546 he had left behind him a vision and an impulse which the present world is just beginning to fully appreciate. We are just beginning to realize that, to be real Protestants, not only must we protest against something, but we must also stand for something with a creative spirit.

Luther's beliefs can be stated as follows:

1. He accepted the old creeds and all their fundamental teachings.

2. His sole authority was the Scriptures. He rejected the special priesthood, and the whole sacramental system of salvation as held by the Roman Catholic Church.

3. Justification by faith was his fundamental belief.

4. He held to baptism, including infant baptism, and baptismal regeneration.

5. He accepted the Lord's Supper, holding that the glorified body and blood of Christ were really present.

6. He believed in heaven and hell, rejecting the doctrine of purgatory.

7. He believed that good works were a necessary fruit of faith.

The Protestant Martyr, Ulrich Zwingli

As Switzerland was nominally a part of Germany at this time, it was quite natural that it should receive the new spirit of reform.

Ulrich Zwingli was born in 1484 of a very good family. After having received his education in the best schools and universities he became a Catholic priest of great power in Zurich. Through a very careful study of the Scriptures he experienced an intellectual conversion and at once set out to reform the Church. It is said that "Luther's principle of reform was the retention in the Church of everything which the Scriptures did not forbid"; while "Zwingli's was the rejection of all that the Scriptures did not warrant." In 1523 the Canton of Zurich established a Reformed Church and a little later St. Gall, Basel, and Berne did the same. In 1532 war broke out between the Roman Catholics and the Reformers in which Zwingli was killed. This began what is called the "Wars of Religion," which followed in many other countries.

Zwingli's views were as follows:

1. He rejected such doctrines and practices of the Roman Catholic Church as the priesthood, sacraments, mass, transubstantiation, and purgatory.

2. His sole authority was the Scriptures.

3. Salvation was by grace through faith, and not by the Church.

4. Baptism was only a sign of the Christian covenant and not a means of regeneration. He accepted infant baptism but not its regenerative aspect.

5. The Lord's Supper was a reminder of Christ, but in no sense his real flesh and blood.

6. He believed in heaven and hell in the future life.

"THE PROTESTANT POPE," JOHN CALVIN

John Calvin was born in 1509 at Noyon, France, of a influential family. He received a very fine education and showed remarkable abilities as a student. At an early age he held positions in the Church and at one time prepared for the law. His conversion was sudden and lasting. In 1533 he was arrested as a reformer but escaped to Geneva. There he met the reformer Farel in 1536, who determined to a great extent his future. Remaining at Geneva he soon became its undisputed master.

"From one of the gayest and most reckless cities of Europe, Geneva was transformed into the soberest and most law-abiding and serious city in the world. It was virtually a theocracy. The church completely dominated the life of the entire community."—MCGLOTHIN.

In 1559 he established the University of Geneva, which became the leading theological school of Europe, and sent its graduates to Scotland, Germany, and Italy. Thus Calvinism spread far and wide until it dominated the Protestant thinking of Europe.

As a system of theology it was the most logical, consistent and thorough statement of Christian doctrine ever given to the world; as a way of Christian life, it had many serious shortcomings.

The main beliefs and practices of Calvinism were:

1. God as all powerful.
2. Man as utterly helpless before God.
3. Salvation by election only.
4. A democratic church government.
5. A Christian life, which was stern and somber, ethical and practical, being enforced by strict discipline.
6. Baptism, as a seal as well as a sign of grace. He retained infant baptism, but only for children of Christian parents.
7. Lord's Supper, where Christians received the spiritual flesh and blood of Christ, not the physical, as Luther believed.
8. Heaven and hell as future resting places.

THE ANABAPTISTS

Many of the followers of both Luther and Calvin demanded that the new spirit be carried out to its logical conclusion—to the reëstablishment of apostolic Christianity. This involved such a radical and revolutionary program that all of the reformers shrank from it. The leaders of the "left" therefore broke from the ranks of the reformers and formed a party of their own.

Their first attack was against infant baptism. They declared it to be unscriptural, anti-Christian, the mere invention of man. In its place they put "believers baptism," which involved a second, or adult, baptism. This was why they were called Anabaptists (Rebaptists) by their opponents.

They believed in a purely regenerate membership of the Church, based upon faith and fellowship with God, in the separation of Church and State, in religious democracy, and in the Scriptures as sole authority. They opposed war and refused to bear arms or to pay war taxes; they refused to take an oath; they objected to capital punishment, to the trade in alcoholic liquors, and to the lending of money at interest by Christians.

They were persecuted by both Catholics and Protestants, and thousands perished at the hands of their Christian brothers, because of the radical faith which they held. Some of them had gone to excess in their social and political practices. But on the whole "they were a harmless people whose chief offenses were their piety and their religious views." And although they were killed in the flesh, their spirit still lived.

PROTESTANT GROWTH

Calvinism made a deep impression in Holland, Scotland, and England. As the result of the victories of William of Orange over Philip II of Spain, Holland became a "reformed" people with an established Calvinistic Church under whose régime the country has flourished. Scotland, under the leadership of John Knox, became a Calvinistic country in 1560, when the Scottish Parliament formally adopted the reform. The national church was called "Presbyterian," which became legally established under James, the son of Mary Stuart. The Anabaptist influence was very strong in England and gave rise to the Puritan movement from which many of our modern denominations have arisen. For a while Calvinism developed in France, but the Catholic opposition was too great. Thousands of Protestants were "butchered" by the Catholics on St. Bartholomew's night, in 1572. For a while the Protestants enjoyed peace under the Edict of Nantes, granted by Henry IV in 1598. But in 1685 persecution again broke out, the Edict was revoked, and the Protestant cause in France suffered a blow from which it has never recovered.

The "Wars of Religion" increased as the Protestants grew in number. The first war has just been mentioned under Henry III, that of Switzerland (1529 to 1531). In 1547 the Schmalkald War broke out in Germany, followed in 1551 by another in which the Protestants completely defeated the Catholics. During 1562 to 1598 both France and the Netherlands were being torn to pieces by religious wars. The most terrible of all wars of religion was the Thirty Years' War in Germany. Not only was Germany devastated by it, but France, England, and Sweden also suffered. It was ended by the famous Treaty of Westphalia. This treaty marks the point where the Catholics were ready to admit that they could never suppress the Protestants by the use of force. While the struggle between Protestants and Roman Catholics has continued ever since, in many different forms all over the world, it has taken place mainly in the arena of theology, and not upon the battle-field.

> Much remains
> To conquer still; peace hath her victories,
> No less renowned than war; new foes arise,
> Threatening to bind our souls with secular chains.
> Help us to save free conscience from the paw
> Of hireling wolves, whose gospel is their maw.
>
> JOHN MILTON

HELPS FOR STUDY

Written Work

1. What happened during the Renaissance?
2. Why is Martin Luther so famous?
3. What did Zwingli believe?
4. How did John Calvin differ from Martin Luther?
5. Who were the Anabaptists?
6. Tell about the Protestant growth.

Oral Discussion

1. Did Luther always do just the right thing?
2. In what sense was Calvin really a Protestant pope?
3. Are wars of religion, or any other kind of warfare, ever Christian?
4. What is the real meaning of Protestantism?

Special Assignments

1. Discover ten facts about Savonarola.
2. Write a brief account of the life of Erasmus.
3. Write an essay showing the importance of William Tyndale.
4. Study the life of Philip Melancthon.
5. Give date, place of birth, and chief contribution of the following men: Copernicus, Galileo, Kepler, Newton, and Francis Bacon.

A REBELLION

. . . the Reformation in England

Let us play the man today, Master Ridley, for by the grace of God we shall light such a fire in England as shall never be put out.—BISHOP LATIMER.

CHARACTER OF THE ENGLISH REFORMATION

The Reformation in England took seed when Wycliffe, in the fourteenth century, began to preach against the temporal and spiritual supremacy of the pope. As a result of the new learning of the Renaissance, there arose a group of great men known as the Oxford Reformers: Colet, Dean of St. Paul's; Thomas More; and Erasmus, the cosmopolitan. These men had become indignant because of the ignorance and immorality of the clergy and desired to enlighten both the clergy and the laity. It was an easy matter to make all patriotic Englishmen see their situation—vassals of the pope, both in civil and sacred matters. They had rebelled many times before, but as yet they were not free from the Roman yoke.

Henry VIII gave England the honor of being the first nation to break away from medievalism and sever all relationships with the ecclesiastical empire of Rome. No revival or reformation of religion, however took place. The Church remained the same; it had merely cut off its official head. The spirit of the Reformation did not really enter the Church until the reign of Edward VI, when he made many radical changes both in doctrine and in practice.

A King Plays Pope

The pope had been considerate to Henry VIII and permitted him to marry Catherine of Aragon, his brother's widow. The king, therefore, supported the pope and became known as the "defender of the faith." But in 1527 Henry desired a divorce. Because the pope was slow in granting it, he decided to adopt the suggestion of Thomas Cromwell that the universities of Europe decide the question. The learned faculties met and, with due regard for the tender conscience of Henry, declared the marriage between Henry and Catherine invalid. Having received this decision, the king resolved to defy and repudiate the supreme authority of the pope. In 1531 he established certain courts which granted him a legal divorce. His marriage to Catherine was then declared null and void by the Archbishop of Canterbury.

In 1534 Parliament declared: that the king was head of the Church in England; that Princess Mary, daughter of Catherine, was illegitimate; that Princess Elizabeth, daughter of Anne Boleyn, the new wife of the king, was in the line of succession; and that all those who refused to accept the "Act of Succession" or to acknowledge the new title and prerogatives of the King were under the jurisdiction of the "Treason Act," which provided punishment by death. As a result of this last law, Sir Thomas More, the Lord Chancelor, was put to death, since he would not confirm the marriage of the king to Anne Boleyn.

The first "service" which Henry performed for the Church was to suppress all monasteries and to confiscate their property. His aim was, not to reform the Church, but to obtain ready money, for he had squandered much in loose living and was financially embarrassed. Therefore the properties were sold in the open market to the highest bidder. Many a noble family of England can trace its birth to this bargain sale.

Through the influence of Cranmer, Archbishop of Canterbury, and Thomas Cromwell, the king's political adviser (both holding secret sympathies with the reformed doctrines of Luther and Zwingli), a short creed called the "Ten Articles" was published (1536) and approved by the king and Convocation. It could scarcely be called a Protestant creed, for it held very closely to the Catholic faith and has been described as "Romish" with the pope left out in the cold. A year later Cranmer drew up the *Bishop's Book,* which contained a much more Protestant doctrine than the "Ten Articles." The following year he constructed another creed, called the "Thirteen Articles," which was based very largely upon the Augsburg Confession, but this did not meet with the king's approval, and the persistent Cranmer lost all favor with the king. In 1539 Henry published the "Six Articles," for the abolishing of diversity of opinion, which resulted in a great deal of persecution. Many called it the "bloody statute" and the "whip with six strings." But fortunately for the nation, the king died in 1547.

EDWARD, THE FAVORITE OF PROTESTANTISM

Henry had left three children: Mary, the daughter of Catherine; Elizabeth, daughter of Anne Boleyn; and Edward, the son of Jane Seymour. Edward became the new king.

From the very first Edward began a program of restoration for the Church. He ordered a Royal Visitation of all the churches to see if their services were conducted properly. He ordered that Cranmer's *Book of Homilies* and Erasmus' *Paraphrase of the New Testament* should be used in public worship. Parliament abolished the Six Articles and the First Prayer Book of Edward VI was adopted. His two advisers, Cheke and Cox, were reformers. As a result of an alliance with Continental Protestantism, doctrinal discussions took place which were colored very largely with Calvinism. In 1553 the Forty-two Articles were published, and in nearly all points they are the same as the Thirty-nine Articles of the present Church of England.

Just as things began to look well for Protestantism, Edward VI died of consumption and "the greatest moan was made for him as ever was heard or seen."

IN BLOODY HANDS AGAIN

Princess Mary, daughter of Catherine, now became Queen of England. She was a rigid Roman Catholic, and her greatest desire was to revenge the wrongs done to her mother. Thinking that the Reformation was the cause for all these wrongs, she set out to destroy it and restore Romanism in England. She abolished the *Prayer Book* and all the changes in worship which had been introduced under the reign of Edward. Cranmer protested against the Queen attending Mass and was sent to the Tower. Later, three hundred others met a similar fate, including such distinguished victims as Ridley, Latimer, and Hooper.

Mary strengthened the Roman yoke by marrying Philip of Spain. He was a loyal Catholic, and through his influence Parliament passed a resolution favoring the reunion with Rome. On St. Andrew's Day, 1554, England received the solemn absolution of the pope and was restored to the communion of the Holy Church. An attempt to restore the Church lands was made, but this was found to be quite impossible.

Mary died in 1558 of dropsy, a heartbroken woman, known as "bloody Mary" by her people. Her persecutions had made the Reformation heroic, and many a young man died in order that his countrymen might be saved from the Roman iron hand. John Rogers, for example, welcomed the honor so much "that he seemed to be going to his marriage." England was to pass into a new day in a new world.

> Ye who bear on the torch of living art
> In this new world saved from some wondrous fate—
> Deem not that ye have come, alas, too late,
> But haste right forward with unfailing heart!
> Ye shall not rest forlorn,—
> Behold, even now, the morn
> Rises in splendor from the Orient sea,
> And the new world shall greet a new divinity.
>
> RICHARD WATSON GILDER

ELIZABETH RESTORES PROTESTANTISM

When Elizabeth came to the throne, England was in a woeful condition. The treasury was empty, a war with France was taking place, the legitimacy of Elizabeth was questioned, and the strength of Protestantism was doubtful. Spain seemed to be friendly and Philip II offered himself in marriage to Elizabeth; but since the marriage depended upon the approval and favor of the pope, the Queen refused. She had therefore chosen to be a Protestant and throw herself upon the sympathies of the English people.

Among the important events of Elizabeth's reign are the following:

1. Repeal of the Romanist legislation.
2. The restoration of royal supremacy over the Church.
3. The restoration of the *Second Prayer Book* of Edward VI with a few alterations.
4. The Act of Uniformity (1559), which compelled all clergymen to use the *Prayer Book* and all people to attend church under penalty of censure and fine unless having a "lawful or reasonable excuse."
5. The revision of the Forty-two Articles of Edward VI resulting in the Thirty-nine Articles (1563) which at the present time constitute the creed of the Anglican Church.
6. The rise of Nonconformity.

Elizabeth, however, did not wholly approve of the Reformation. She desired to have the Church retain images, crucifixes, holy water, and the celibacy of the clergy, but she was compelled to accept the Calvinist theory of the Lord's Supper.

It was the royal supremacy of Elizabeth, enforced through the Court of High Commission, which prepared the way for the Puritan revolt under Charles I and for Black Bartholomew's Day under Charles II. Had the Church of England been left to its own spiritual instincts, unthwarted by Erastian control, both those calamities might have been spared it.—T. M. LINDSAY.

PURITANISM

Puritanism does not stand for any one sect but was the name given to all those Protestants in England, from the time of Elizabeth onward, who held to the Calvinistic doctrines and practices. The most powerful stimulant to this movement was the new English translation of the Bible (King James's Version of the Bible, 1611). The people became filled with its spirit and message.

This movement demanded a purity of life, a revision of the *Prayer Book*, simplicity in worship, and a presbyterian form of government in Church affairs. It also brought about our "English Sunday" and the peculiarly British practice of family prayer.) Some of the outstanding leaders of Puritan thought and practice were Strickland, Peter Wentworth, John Milton, John Bunyan, John Fox, and Oliver Cromwell. As a whole, Puritanism represented the best in English life and thought.

In 1642, the Puritan Revolution was finally precipitated and Charles I was overthrown and beheaded. For a while the government was in the hands of Cromwell, but on the accession of Charles II the Church of England was reestablished and all the other forms of religious worship were suppressed. Although Puritanism as a movement disappeared, its spirit lived on and was reincarnated in many independent bodies which arose during this period.

HELPS FOR STUDY

Written Work

1. What was the character of the English Reformation?
2. How did Henry VIII influence the Reformation?
3. What reforms did Edward VI make?
4. What was the purpose of Mary and how successful was she in carrying it out?
5. Was Elizabeth's reign a strengthening factor to Protestantism?
6. What did Puritanism stand for?

Oral Discussion

1. Will people die for their religion today?
2. How does the organization of a church affect one's belief?
3. What is the trouble with Protestantism today?
4. Were the Puritans good Christians?

Special Assignments

1. Study the Roman Catholic viewpoint of the Reformation. (See *History of the Protestant Reformation*, by Cobbett.)

2. Write a brief account of the lives of John Milton and John Bunyan.

3. Locate one of Milton's poems which reflects the Puritan spirit.

4. Study the Belgic Confession (1561) and the Heidelberg Catechism (1563).

5. Tell what happened on St. Bartholomew's night (1572).

6. Look up some facts concerning the following men: Descartes, Pascal, Leibnitz, and Spinoza.

· 17 ·

SOMETHING NEW

. . . the Results of the Reformation

Give me liberty, to know, to utter, and to argue freely according to conscience, above all liberties.—JOHN MILTON.

THE RISE OF DENOMINATIONS

The strict laws and practices of the Puritans resulted in a great reaction under Charles II (1630 to 1685). In the first place the Act of Uniformity (1662) compelled almost two thousand Puritan clergymen to withdraw from the Church of England. Conventicle and Five-mile Acts were passed which deprived the Nonconformists of their special forms of worship. It was not until 1689 that they were granted their freedom by the passage of the Toleration Act, in the reign of William and Mary. Meanwhile many different sects had grown up.

The Quakers. The denomination known as the Friends, or Quakers, was founded by George Fox (1624 to 1691). When he was nineteen, so he tells us, the Lord said to him, after he had returned from a wild party:

Thou seest how young people go together unto vanity and old people unto the earth; thou must forsake all, both young and old, and keep out of all, and be a stranger unto all.

He took this advice, and by means of an "inner light" the Scriptures were opened to him; thereafter he used this enlightenment for salvation and for spiritual guidance. In 1666 the Society of Friends was organized. It had no churches (only "meeting houses"), no ministers, and no set service. The members met in silence and did not speak until moved to do so by the spirit. Their central belief was that: "The Divine Being speaks directly to the heart of every man." This voice was called the "Light of Christ," "Word of God," "Christ Within," the "Seed," or "Grace." They were all addressed as "thee," for they made no distinction between people or between the two sexes. They refused to join armies or to take any kind of oath, and they would doff their hat to no man—not even the king. These beliefs and practices caused them to be severely persecuted and it is estimated that from 1650 to 1689 as many as fourteen thousand of them were imprisoned, while several hundred either died in prison or were killed. But this brave little society could not be annihilated so easily.) In a later chapter of this book (Chapter XXVI), the Friends will be discussed more at length, especially in their relation to America.

Congregationalism. Congregationalism was founded by Robert Browne, a young Cambridge student, who had learned the Anabaptist view in Holland. In 1580 he separated from the Church of England and set up a democratic church at Norwich, but he was untrue to his original ideals and the church finally broke up. Later, at Gainsborough and Scrooby, another church was set up by John Smyth and John Robinson, but it was soon driven to the continent and, in 1607, settled in Holland. In 1620 a large part of John Robinson's congregation came to America in the *Mayflower* and not only founded New England but also American Congregationalism.

The English Baptists. As a denomination, the English Baptists date from 1611 when a group of John Smyth's congregation, while still in Holland, broke relations with the Independents and returned to England under the leadership of Henry Helwys and John Morton. They insisted on believers baptism, religious freedom, the salvation of all infants dying in infancy, and an open Bible. Although severely persecuted they claimed to have 20,000 members in 1660. A little later a sect called the "English Calvinistic (or Particular) Baptists" arose, and then the "General Baptists." The Baptists were first represented in

America by Roger Williams, who founded the first Baptist church in Providence in 1638.

THE ROMAN CATHOLIC CHURCH REFORMS

To keep abreast of the times the Roman Catholic Church realized that it must reform and thus regain its former power. So Paul III summoned a General Council to be held at Trent on December 15, 1545. Here doctrines of the Church were defined, justification by faith condemned, the Church made equal to the Bible as an authority, the sale of indulgences abolished, and education for the clergy stressed. The Scriptures were translated into the vernacular, with special notes, and sent into many different countries. (Yet the old Latin Vulgate still remained the authentic version.) The moral life was also emphasized, which resulted later in a better and higher type of clergy.

Two results of this Council were of great importance to the Roman Catholic Church. In the first place a Catechism was compiled which summed up all Catholic doctrine in very precise terms and, in the second place, the famous Index, which consisted of a list of books which all Catholics were forbidden to read, was created. Now the Roman Catholic Church, with these new weapons and the new-formed order of Jesuits, was ready to make another attempt at world domination.

THE CATHOLIC "MINUTE MEN"

Ignatius Loyola, a Spanish nobleman, was injured in both legs at the siege of Pampeluna (1523). While he was recovering from the wounds he conceived the plan of forming a monastic order composed of military men who would be at the service of the Church. At the University of Paris he gathered a group of men and set out for the Holy Land to do missionary work. But the road was blocked and, returning to Rome, the "Society of Jesus" was organized. Members took the regular monastic vows, and in addition they took the vow to go wherever the Church willed on a moment's notice. They were militant in spirit and action, having a general at Rome and officers throughout the world. The society soon became the controlling force of the papacy and by using its powerful weapons of missions—the confessional, education, and force—it sought to control the destinies of nations. Its influence became so great that both the ecclesiastical and the civil authorities of the Catholic Church came to fear it and demanded its suppression. In 1773 it was finally suppressed and dissolved by Clement XIV, thus leaving him to do as he pleased. But the Society of Jesus was restored in 1814 by Pius VII and played its part in the revival of the Church in the nineteenth century.

The Protestants Seek Freedom

The Conventicle Act of 1592 had driven the Separatists out of England and threatened them with death if they returned. Most of these refugees made their new homes in Amsterdam, Holland, where they were welcomed and allowed to worship as they saw fit. During the period of 1595 to 1620 many of these companies went to Holland, including such men as Henry Ainsworth, Francis Johnson, and John Robinson. The next chapter will deal with the Pilgrims, who left Holland to settle in the land of freedom. Mrs. Hemans truly describes them when she sings:

> Not as the conqueror comes,
>   They, the true-hearted, came;
> Not with the roll of the stirring drums,
>   And the trumpet that sings of fame.

> There were men with hoary hair
>   Amidst that pilgrim band:
> Why had they come to wither there,
>   Away from their childhood's land?

HELPS FOR STUDY

Written Work

1. What gave rise to denominations?
2. Tell why George Fox founded the Society of Friends and give some of their beliefs and practices.

3. What connection has English Congregationalism with the settling of America?

4. How was the Baptist denomination founded?

5. What were some of the reforms of the Catholic Church?

6. Who were the Jesuits and how powerful were they?

7. Where did the Protestants go to seek freedom?

Oral Discussion

1. Does the rise of denominations serve to justify the importance that we place on them today?

2. Should we ever compromise our ideals or standards in order to be sociable or agreeable?

3. Can one who takes his Christianity seriously be popular today?

4. Would it not have been better to have reformed the Roman Catholic Church from within than to have so many different denominations?

Special Assignments

1. Write a short account of the Inquisition and the Thirty Years' War.

2. Prepare a paper on "What John Wesley Means to the Methodist Church."

3. Make a study of the life of George Whitefield.

·18·

THE CHURCH IN NORTH AMERICA

Then, pale and worn, he paced his deck,
And peered through darkness—Ah, that night
Of all dark nights. And then a speck—
A light! A light! A light! A light!
It grew, a scarlet flag unfurled!
It grew to be Time's burst of dawn.
He gained a world; he gave that world
Its grandest lesson: On! Sail on!

JOAQUIN MILLER

MISSIONS

Columbus' discovery of America (1492) gave to the Church a new hope—that of Christian missions. As Daniel Webster said: "It cannot be denied that with America and in America a new era commences in human affairs." All Europe wanted a share in this new and rich land. Spain sent out expeditions under such men as Ponce de Leon, Balboa, Cortez, DeSoto, and Coronado; English expeditions were led by Frobisher, Davis, Gilbert, and Raleigh; and the French made explorations along the St. Lawrence River, led by Jacques Cartier. In all these discoveries the Church had a large part. This was the period when England and Spain were bitter rivals. England, during Elizabeth's reign, was making a brave fight for the Protestant cause, while Spain under Philip II was still loyal to the pope. With every expedition from Spain, therefore, and also from Portugal and from France, a priest went in the name of the Church; in every English expedition a representative of the

129

Church of England was included. As Henry Rowe writes, in his *History of Religion in the United States:*

Spanish noblemen took with them their Catholic priests to plant the banner of the Cross alongside the banner of Spain, for their religion was a part of the equipment of their Latin civilization. . . . A century later French voyageurs into Canada took with them their confessors, and the devoted Jesuit missionaries pushed into the interior to propagate their faith among the natives of the North.

TRANSPLANTING DENOMINATIONS

As a result of the Reformation there sprang up, all through Europe, many sects or denominations. When immigrants came to America from different parts of Europe they brought with them their own particular belief. When the Dutch emigrated to New Netherlands, they took their Reformed Church with them; when Sweden sent her emigrants to Delaware, she also sent the Lutheran Church with them; when England established a permanent settlement in Virginia, she also established the Church of England along with it. A little later English Puritanism found a place in New England, and the Presbyterians and Baptists established themselves in Maryland, Virginia, and the Carolinas. The English Quakers bought New Jersey, and the Methodists were found in America before they separated from the Church of England. And in America these denominations found rich soil in which to grow.

VIRGINIA, THE NEW HOME OF THE CHURCH OF ENGLAND

It was in 1607 that English immigrants settled in Jamestown, Virginia. At first these colonists met with defeat on every hand, but with the help of their dauntless leader, John Smith, they finally won a measure of success.

This colony was governed by a body which was subject to a council in England under the control of the king. This council saw to it that the colonists did not forget their Mother Church. One article in the charter read "that the colonists should establish the Church of England as the only form of worship," and the governors saw that this was carried out. It is said that if a man refused to go to church he was put on a short allowance of victuals, and then whipped every day until he begged to hear the preaching once more. It must have been wonderful to be a preacher in those days!

This system, however, did not prove satisfactory. It was too far removed from the Mother Church to work effectively. Also it lacked a bishop to confirm the young people and to ordain a native clergy. As the colonists were democratic in spirit this control was a great hindrance to their growth. As Henry Rowe says:

> Far better it would have been to throw the colonial churches on their own responsibility, permitting them to grow vigorous through self-reliance.

New England Congregationalism

The Separatists, having withdrawn from the Church of England because of its form of worship, had formed independent congregations. Since they were not able to obtain freedom in England, they went to Holland (1607). Here they found a welcome, but realizing that they would soon lose their very language and customs if they remained, they decided to emigrate to America. On December 21, 1620, the good ship *Mayflower* sailed into Plymouth, Massachusetts, harbor with one hundred and two Pilgrims. It was not long before they had built log huts for general use, had their own government, had laws and were enforcing them, made treaties with the Indians, bought out the English company, farmed, fished, and traded. And so the colony grew. "Sunday after Sunday they climbed the hill to the log church, which was at once meeting-house, fort, lookout; lived as good neighbors during the week; and acknowledged no ecclesiastical authority but their own suffrages."

In this manner Congregationalism was planted in America—being the first denomination to break away from the old ecclesiastical order in the new land of freedom. Their courage and foresight paved the way for Puritan New England which gave to America its first lessons in stern justice, moral living, and aggressive business methods.

PURITANISM IN AMERICA

In 1630, a great emigration of Puritans to New England began under the direction of the Massachusetts Bay Company. John Winthrop, a wealthy Puritan, was made governor, and he with seven hundred of his kinsmen settled in and around Boston. During the next ten years 20,000 others followed and were "the very flower of the English Puritans." This colony had its own town meetings which Thomas Jefferson said were the "wisest invention ever devised by the wit of man for the perfect exercise of self-government." (Only members of the Puritan Church could vote.) Soon these people became engaged in fishing and ship-building, and thriving commerce with the West Indies resulted.

These people believed in education and said that "learning should not be buried in the graves of their fathers." In 1635 the Boston Free Latin School was built, the oldest English school in America. By 1647 the foundation of the common-school system in the United States had been laid by the Puritans. It was in 1639 that the first English college was founded: Harvard College, at Cambridge, Massachusetts. This began the line of Puritan institutions which was to extend across America.

According to Peabody:

Puritanism, intolerant and severe as it often was, made its direct appeal to the individual conscience and the experience of the soul. It forfeited many pleasures, but it delighted in God. It created what has been called a hard church.

But it saved America the fate of having a soft church. Great were the contributions of the Puritans to America. It might be for the total welfare of Protestantism today to have a little more of the moral backbone of Puritanism.

RELIGIOUS EMANCIPATION

The Puritans had demonstrated the value of religious freedom, even if they had not always practiced it. After all, they had gone only half way. It was left to Roger Williams to emancipate religion in America. He was the first person to put into practice the American principle, "that government has nothing whatever to do with maintaining any particular form of religious worship."

Having been driven from Massachusetts because of his religious views Roger Williams fled to the south with a few of his friends and settled in a land he called "Providence." Here he formed a colony which granted liberty to all, whether they were Protestants, Catholics, or Jews. It even protected unbelievers just as long as they behaved themselves. This idea of freedom grew gradually, although it was at first feared by the other colonies, until it became written into the Constitution of the United States in these words:

Congress shall make no law respecting an establishment of religion, or prohibiting the free exercise thereof.

No religious test shall ever be required as a qualification to any office or public trust under the United States.

History has honored Roger Williams by placing him in the ranks with Newton, Kepler, and Copernicus, as a modern benefactor to mankind. This is only a fair estimate of his worth when his contribution to America is considered.

HELPS FOR STUDY

Written Work

1. Give an account of the early missionary activities in America.
2. How were denominations transplanted?
3. Why was not the Church of England entirely successful in America?
4. Give an account of New England Congregationalism.
5. Who were the Puritans?
6. What did Roger Williams do?

Oral Discussion

1. What great lesson did Columbus teach the world?

2. Does the missionary usually blaze the trail for the State?

3. In what areas of the world are the issues between Church and State still being fought out?

4. Has America always stood for the principles upon which it was first founded?

Special Assignments

1. Tell the story of the Pilgrims.

2. Write a brief account of the life of Roger Williams.

3. Show how the Church in America provided a working model of democratic government.

· 19 ·

THE CHURCH OF AUTHORITY
... the Roman Catholic Church[1]

There never was on this earth a work of human policy so well deserving of careful study as the Roman Catholic Church.—THOMAS B. MACAULAY.

WHEN?

It hardly seems necessary to answer the question "When?" for one who has read thus far. We have been dealing altogether with the Roman Catholic Church from the time of the first century to the Reformation. The history of this Church may be traced through the successive bishoprics of Rome, from Peter until the present day. This is the Church which recognizes the Pope as the vicar of Christ on earth and the visible head of the Church. Chapter IV to XVI give the reader a brief outline of its early history.

WHERE?

The Roman Catholic Church was founded at Rome, which seemed to be the natural location for such an organization, both geographically and politically. It then extended its power westward, until it had a mighty following throughout all Europe.

Roman Catholic history in America begins about 1125 A.D., when the first diocese was established in Greenland; and there were resident bishops until 1377. It was considered too cold in Greenland for any permanent settlement. A bishop-elect

---

[1] Approximately 24,500,000 members in the United States.

came along with Columbus to the New World. Sees were established in Haiti and Puerto Rico. In 1565 the first parish in the United States proper was founded, that of St. Augustine. Roman Catholic work was also developed about this time in Mexico. Seventy-five years after Columbus, the Roman Catholic Church was well established in America.

Most of the French explorers and colonizers of the sixteenth and seventeenth centuries were Roman Catholics. Missionary groups were also active. The vast province of France, which included the Mississippi valley along with Louisiana, came under the jurisdiction of the See of Quebec in 1674.

In 1634 Roman Catholics founded Maryland, which, according to Catholic historians, has the distinction of being the first English settlement where religious freedom was a part of the common law. Jesuits, from 1634 to 1773, worked in Maryland, Pennsylvania, and northern Virginia. In 1784, Father John Carroll was appointed Prefect-Apostolic of the Roman Catholic Church in the United States, and six years later became the first bishop of Baltimore, with jurisdiction over the entire country. From this time on, and particularly from 1828 to World War I, the growth of this Church was exceedingly rapid, owing largely to immigration.

WHY?

The Roman Catholic Church is the continuation in history of the first Apostolic Church. It remained the principal Church of Christianity until the schism in 1054. There has been no break in this organization from the very beginning to the present time, although during the Middle Ages it was shaken by corruption and moral decay. It has always renewed its spirit, however, and today is one of the most powerful and influential factors in the modern world.

WHAT—IN ORGANIZATION?

The Papacy. At the head of the Roman Catholic Church sits the Bishop of Rome, who is Pope. His authority is supreme in all things concerning the Church. Next in order is the College of Cardinals, which acts as an adviser and head of commissions, called congregations. The cardinals elect the new Pope in case of death, and many of them make their home at Rome.

A cardinal secretary at the Vatican serves as Secretary of State. Permanent "congregations," each with a cardinal at its head, consist of The Holy Office, Consistorial, Sacramental Discipline, The Council, Affairs of Religions, de Propaganda Fide. Tribunals control the judicial functions of the Vatican State. Besides the greater prelates—the Archbishops, Metropolitans, and Patriarchs—there are bishops, priests, and deacons. The actual government of the Church here in the United States is represented by an apostolic delegate at Washington, D. C., cardinals, archbishops, bishops, diocesan clergymen, and members of various religious orders. A diocese includes:

1. A bishop.
2. The Cathedral Chapter.
3. A vicar-general.
4. A Diocesan Chancery.
5. Parishes.

Appointments. All appointees to bishoprics in this country are made by the Holy See at Rome, upon the recommendation of the hierarchy in the United States. No married person can hold an office in the Roman Church. Their two main reasons for this are: celibacy leaves them more free to perform their duties, and continence is regarded as a more holy state than marriage.

Income. The income of the Church is derived from pew rents, plate collections, offerings for baptism, marriage ceremonies, masses, etc. All of the money is in charge of the priest, who retains his own salary and the running expenses of the Church, and then places the remainder to the credit of the Church.

The priest's salary is fixed by each diocese and is uniform throughout the diocese.

Church Services. The different services of the Roman Catholic Church are as follows:

1. *High Mass,* celebrated at 10 A.M. and noon on Sundays.
    a. Parts of the liturgy are sung by the officiating clergymen, and other parts by the choir.
    b. A sermon is delivered by one of the priests.
2. *Low Mass,* celebrated from 5 A.M. until 10 A.M. on Sundays.
    a. Mass is read.
    b. Short instruction is given.
3. *Vespers,* sung on Sunday afternoon or evening.
4. *Mass,* said daily by the priest.
5. *Special services,* held on Fridays and on all holy days.

WHAT—IN BELIEF?

Since it is impossible to do justice to the history, practices, and doctrines of the Roman Catholic Church in such a limited amount of space as we have available here, we would strongly recommend that the reader secure such leaflets and booklets as the following, which give, in semi-popular form, the position of this Church: *Introduction to Catholicism,* by Martin J. Scott; *Sixteen Steps to the Church; Five Great Encyclicals; The Faith of Our Fathers,* by James Cardinal Gibbons; and *The Faith of Millions,* by the Reverend Dr. John A. O'Brien. Also a reading of *My Sunday Missal* helps to give an understanding of the devotional side of Roman Catholicism.

These few quotations from the Catechism give a fairly good idea of what Roman Catholics are taught concerning:

The Virgin Mary. Original sin is not actual, but inherited. Our first parents, by their transgression of God's commandments, lost their high estate. . . . The Blessed Virgin Mary alone, of all human persons, was exempt from original sin, that is, from the first moment of conception, she possessed justice and holiness, namely, fulness of grace. That is the meaning of the Immaculate Conception.

Incarnation. The Incarnation means that the Son of God became man in the course of time. Christ was God from all eternity, and Man from the time of His human birth. When it is said that God became man, it does not mean that He was changed into man, but that as God, He assumed human nature, so that in the one person Christ, there are the two natures, the divine and the human. This, like the Trinity, is a mystery of faith.

The Church. The Church is the congregation of all those who profess the faith of Christ, partake of the same sacraments, and are governed by their lawful pastors under one visible Head.

The Pope. The Pope is the visible head of the Church of which Christ is the invisible head. The Pope when defining matters of faith and morals, has Christ's guarantee that he will not err. This prerogative of the Pope is called Papal Infallibility. It is divine assurance that when the Pope in his official capacity, declares and defines Christian dogma, he is immune from error.

The Sacraments. There are seven sacraments: Baptism, Confirmation, Holy Eucharist, Penance, Extreme Unction, Holy Orders, and Matrimony. . . . A sacrament is an outward sign instituted by Christ to give grace. . . . The sacraments are not mere symbols, but actually bestow grace, and hence were instituted by Christ Himself, the possessor and origin of grace. No human being has the power to institute a sacrament.

Baptism. Baptism is the first and the most necessary of the sacraments. . . . Besides remitting sin, Baptism confers sanctifying grace, making the baptized person a child of God. By Baptism, all our sins, original and actual, are forgiven; all punishment due to sin is remitted; our souls receive a mark or character which will remain forever.

Forgiveness of Sins. By the sacrament of Penance, Christ conferred on His Church the power to forgive sins: "Whose sins you shall forgive, they are forgiven them" (John XX, 23). By the absolution and penance given after confession, the guilt and eternal punishment of sin are remitted, and also part of the temporal punishment.

Transubstantiation. By the Consecration at Mass, the substance of bread and wine becomes the Body and Blood of Christ. This change is termed Transubstantiation. . . . Ordinarily when the substance of a thing changes, there is a corresponding change of the accidents. But in the case of the Eucharist, the externals or accidents do not change with the change of substance. We have no perceptible evidence of the change. We believe it on the word of God. Hence the Eucharist is called a mystery of faith.

The Mass. The Mass is the renewal of the sacrifice of the Cross in an unbloody manner, the same as the first Mass, celebrated in anticipation, by Christ Himself at the Last Supper.

Extreme Unction. Extreme Unction is so called because it is administered as the last rite to the faithful. Like all the sacraments, it confers grace through the infinite merits of Jesus Christ. The dispositions of the recipient may affect more or less the spiritual benefits of Extreme Unction, but the grace of the sacrament is conferred even on those who are unconscious, provided they had the intention, at least implicitly, of receiving this sacrament with the proper dispositions when the necessity should arise.

Holy Orders. Holy Orders is the sacrament instituted by Christ in order to perpetuate the ministry of His Church. By this sacrament, bishops, priests and other clerics receive the power and grace to perform the sacred duties of their various ministries. The Catholic priesthood goes back in unbroken and valid succession to Christ Himself. The Catholic priesthood, alone, recognizes the successor of Peter as the Vicar of Christ, the Chief Bishop of Christendom, the Rock on which the Church of Christ rests divinely secure.

HELPS FOR STUDY

Written Work

1. When and where was the Roman Catholic Church founded in America?

2. What is the organization of this Church?

3. Explain the different types of services of this Church.

4. Name the seven sacraments.

5. What do the following terms mean: baptism, confirmation, purgatory, penance, the eucharist, marriage?

Oral Discussion

1. What holds the Roman Catholics to their faith?

2. How does the form of worship affect the spirit of worship?

3. Is the Roman Catholic Church the only true Church?

4. Does the Roman Catholic Church seek world dominion?

5. What reasons are given for having official relationships between the Vatican and the United States Government?

6. Should saints be worshiped?

7. Should public tax money be used to support sectarian schools?
8. What is the influence of this Church at the present time?

Special Assignments

1. How many Roman Catholics are there in the United States? In the world?

2. Make a list of the most prominent Catholics in history.

3. Give the strength and the weakness of this Church.

4. Outline Chapter VIII of Brown's *The Larger Faith*.

5. Make a map showing the parts of the world where Catholic influence is the strongest at the present time.

THE CHURCH OF BEAUTY

... the Protestant Episcopal Church[1]

A thing of beauty is a joy for ever:
Its loveliness increases; it will never
Pass into nothingness; but still will keep
A bower quiet for us, and a sleep
Full of sweet dreams, and health, and quiet breathing.

JOHN KEATS

Brown, in *The Larger Faith,* in speaking of the Protestant Episcopal Church, says:

It seeks to develop gentlemen and gentlewomen. The saturative influence of good architecture, of tasteful interiors, of good stained glass, where the colors do not eat each other up, of a finely framed liturgy, of noble music and of the spirit of decorum in worship.

WHEN AND WHERE?

The Church of England was first planted in America by a chaplain of the exploring expeditions of Frobisher (1578) and Drake (1579). The charters, which Sir Humphrey Gilbert (1578) and Sir Walter Raleigh (1584 to 1587) had, provided for "public service according to the Church of England." Permanent worship was begun in 1607 by the Reverend Robert Hunt, at Jamestown, Virginia, when he celebrated the eucharist beneath a large sail stretched between two trees. At first toleration was shown to all, but as the Crown secured direct control

---

[1] Approximately 2,200,000 members in the United States.

over the colony harsh and rigid laws were prevalent in regard to Puritans and Quakers.

The first Episcopal Church in New England was King's Chapel in Boston, opened in 1689. During 1698 a church was established at Newport, Rhode Island, and also the Trinity Church in New York City was consecrated the same year.

There were two weaknesses in these first churches in America: first, there were only a few established churches in the colonies and these aroused antagonism, for the colonists had no desire for a State-Church; and, in the second place, it was not possible to obtain competent ministers because of the fact that they had to go to England to be ordained. Thus it was very difficult for the Mother Church to keep watchful care over the younger churches in America.

Samuel Seabury became the first bishop of the American Church in 1784. Elected to the office by the clergy of Connecticut, he was consecrated by the Scottish Episcopal Church. "Seabury House," headquarters of the present national organization, is named after him.

The first move toward independence was made in 1782, when the Reverend William White of Philadelphia published "The Case of the Episcopal Churches in the United States Considered," which urged the churches to form some kind of an organization. The name "Protestant Episcopal" was first proposed by a committee at Annapolis in 1783 and adopted by the General Convention of 1789. The term "Protestant" was to distinguish it from the Church of Rome, and the word "Episcopal" was to distinguish it from the Presbyterian and the Congregational bodies. In the same year the *Book of Common Prayer*, the constitution, and canons were adopted.

The name of Dr. W. A. Muhlenberg should be mentioned in relation to this Church.

He founded the system of Church schools, organized the first free church of any importance in New York City, introduced the male choir, sisterhoods, and the fresh air movement; while his church infirmary suggested to his mind St. Luke's Hospital, the first church hospital of any Christian communion in the country.

The Protestant Episcopal Church has always been very active in the ecumenical movement and has contributed many outstanding public servants. Her missionary work has been a strong factor in the development of central administrative organizations. It also takes care of large areas of social service and community welfare work.

WHY?

The Protestant Episcopal Church is in the main the Church of England reborn in America. During the colonial period it was under the jurisdiction of the Bishop of London, but after the War of the Revolution it formed its own organization and became separate from the Mother Church. Yet, as the preface to the American *Prayer Book* states:

This Church is far from intending to depart from the Church of England in any essential point of doctrine, discipline, or worship.

WHAT—IN ORGANIZATION?

System of Government. This includes the parish, the diocese, the National Council, and the General Convention.

Officers of Parish. The officers consist of a rector, who is also a priest; the wardens, who have charge of all records and the collection of alms; and vestrymen, who have charge of the church property.

The Diocese. The government of the diocese rests upon the bishop and the diocesan convention, which meets annually. This convention is a self-governing body, but appoints a standing committee for all purposes declared by the General Convention. A bishop is elected by the diocese, but must be approved by a majority of the bishops and the standing committees of all the dioceses.

The General Convention. This is the highest ecclesiastical authority in the Church. It consists of the House of Deputies, which is composed of delegates elected from the dioceses; and the House of Bishops, which includes:

. . . every bishop having jurisdiction, every bishop coadjutor, and every bishop who by reason of advanced age or bodily infirmity has resigned his jurisdiction.

The two Houses vote and deliberate separately. Every measure which becomes a law must be passed by both Houses.

A National Council was established in 1919, with a presiding bishop at its head. It acts as the executive body of the General Convention between sessions and has charge of general missionary, social, and educational work.

The Rector. The rector is received according to diocesan law. His salary is cared for by the vestry of the local church. Some dioceses have endowment funds from which the salary of the rector is provided. The missionary bishops receive their salaries from the treasury of the Domestic and Foreign Missionary Society.

Lay Readers and Deaconesses. These are appointed by the bishop of a diocese or missionary district, to assist in public services, to care for the poor and sick, and to instruct in religious education.

WHAT—IN BELIEF?

Creeds. The Protestant Episcopal Church adopts the Apostles' Creed and the Nicene Creed.

It expects of all its members loyalty to the doctrine, discipline, and worship of the one holy Catholic Apostolic Church, in all the essentials, but allows great liberty in non-essentials. There is no inclination to be rigid or to raise difficulties, but the fundamental principles of the church, based upon the Holy Scripture as the ultimate rule of faith, have been maintained whenever a question has arisen demanding decision.

Clergy. The clergy make the following declaration:

I do believe the Holy Scripture of the Old and New Testaments to be the Word of God, and to contain all things necessary to salvation, and I do solemnly engage to conform to the doctrine, discipline, and worship of the Protestant Episcopal Church in the United States of America.

Baptism. Baptism is by either immersion or pouring. Those who have been baptized as children are received into church membership through confirmation by the bishop, after having been instructed in the catechism of the Church. For those who were not baptized as children, admission is by baptism—either immersion, sprinkling, or pouring—and acceptance of the Apostles' Creed.

Communion. This denomination makes a great deal of the Lord's Supper, the "High Church" holding to a similar view as the Roman Catholics.

The Thirty-nine Articles. The Thirty-nine Articles of the Church of England (with the exception of the twenty-first) were accepted in 1801 as a general statement of doctrine. They are added to the *Prayer Book,* but are not required as essential for either confirmation or ordination.[2]

CHURCH OF ENGLAND IN CANADA

During the war years, along with practical Christian service, there developed a new interest in Christian doctrine and a new emphasis upon Christian faith. The Church of England in Canada, for example, conducted important studies in this general area. The new concern is manifest largely among the clergy, but lay interest is increasing.

The Church of England in Canada has been particularly active in the field of closer co-operation among the Churches. Its General Synod, in 1943, made a proposal to develop a mutually acceptable ministry in its own Church and the United Church of Canada. In a report made in 1946 it is stated: "The ultimate motive behind all the approach of the two Communions to each other is doubtless that, some day, our Lord's prayer for His Church may be visibly realized, 'That they all may be one.' But the immediate and pressing motive is to be found in the

---

[2] Booklets entitled *The Episcopal Church,* by Walter Herbert Stowe; *Tell Us About the National Council;* and *The Episcopal Church, Some Interesting Facts;* may be secured from the National Council, Protestant Episcopal Church, New York City.

manifest needs of Canada for the unifying of the Christian forces of our land, especially in its outlying regions. . . . We suggest that the next steps be toward a ministry recognized by both Communions and toward unity at the Lord's Table."

In 1948 and 1949, the supreme courts of the Church of England in Canada and the United Church of Canada will be asked to consider a plan "whereby any minister of the United Church could receive Holy Orders according to the form and manner of the Church of England in Canada, and any clergyman of the Church of England in Canada could be admitted to the ministry of the United Church of Canada by the appropriate court of that Church and according to the form used in the United Church Book of Common Order. In both cases it would be made clear, by a preface to be read before the service, that in neither case is any man denying the reality of the ministry he has already received and exercised, but that he has a commission for a further ministry, and the necessary grace from God to perform the same."

Like other Canadian churches, the Church of England in Canada has undertaken an extensive postwar program of strengthening its work. It has promoted an Anglican Advance Appeal. It is also concerned with the rising tide of secularism in Canada, along with bad moral and social conditions. In 1946 it received, through its General Synod, an important report on Marriage and Divorce.

The Canadian Youth Commission, which is a private and independent body, reported in 1945 that 89 per cent of young Roman Catholics (15-24 years of age) say they attend church every Sunday, but only 38 per cent of Protestant young people make this claim. The Commission also discovered a large amount of religious illiteracy among Protestant youth. Such conditions are now being gradually corrected through special campaigns of evangelism and Christian education.

Since the Church of England in Canada has common historic connections with the Protestant Episcopal Church, a brief résumé of its present status is presented here. In order, however, to secure a proper appreciation of its position among the denominations, reference should be made to Chapters 15-17.

ACTIVE IN LARGER WORK

The church life of Canada is now centered in the Canadian Council of Churches, which has as constituent members the Church of England in Canada, the Baptist Federation of Canada, the Churches of Christ (Disciples), the Evangelical Church, the Presbyterian Church in Canada, the Ukrainian Orthodox Church, the United Church of Canada, the Salvation Army, and the Society of Friends. The national Y.M.C.A., Y.W.C.A., and the Student Christian Movement are affiliated members. The Evangelical Lutheran Synod cooperates in one of the Council's departments, that of Ecumenical Affairs.

The Council, which was organized in 1944, has active Departments of Evangelism, Ecumenical Affairs, and Social Relations. It has a close association with the World Council of Churches and the International Missionary Council. While it is still in the process of organization it is rendering a large service by promoting common evangelistic efforts, providing a news-broadcasting service, and participating in the program of relief and reconstruction for Europe and Asia.

According to the 1941 census, Canada has a population of 11,506,655. Of the total population 43⅓ per cent are Roman Catholics. The major denominational groups are:

United Church of Canada	19.16%
Church of England in Canada	15.22%
Presbyterian Church in Canada	7.21%
Baptist Churches	4.20%
Lutheran Churches	3.49%

For information about the United Church of Canada (see pp. 217-218).

HELPS FOR STUDY

Written Work

1. Give an outline of the history of the Church of England in America.
2. Why do we have an Episcopal Church in America?
3. What is the organization of this Church?
4. What does it believe?
5. Why is there a Church of England in Canada?

Oral Discussion

1. Why may this Church be called "the Church of beauty"?
2. Why do so many Episcopalians become prominent public servants?
3. What is the difference between the Roman Catholic Church and the Protestant Episcopal Church?
4. How has the Protestant Episcopal Church taken leadership in the ecumenical movement?

Special Assignments

1. Describe the *Prayer Book*.
2. Make a list of the special days in the Church year.
3. Outline Chapter IV in Brown's *The Larger Faith*.
4. Comment upon the following statement:

The most significant contribution the Protestant Episcopal Church is making to the religious life of the United States is that of "an emphasis upon the historical continuity and universality, upon the conception of the Church as the body of Christ, the channel of supernatural grace."

·21·

THE CHURCH OF DUTY
. . . the Presbyterian Church[1]

If e'er when faith had fallen asleep,
I heard a voice, "Believe no more"
And heard an ever-breaking shore
That tumbled in the godless deep;
A warmth within the breast would melt
The freezing reason's colder part,
And like a man in wrath the heart
Stood up and answered "I have felt."

TENNYSON

WHEN AND WHERE?

The first Presbyterian churches in this country were established in Virginia, New England, Maryland, and Delaware. They were mostly of English or Scottish origin. The first established church was in Virginia. It resulted from the appointment of the Reverend Alexander Whitaker as pastor in 1611. There were also many Presbyterians among the first settlers of New England and in the church founded at Plymouth in 1620.

The first ecclesiastical gathering of an intercolonial and federal character was held by this denomination at Philadelphia in 1706. Here was formed a presbytery, but in 1716 the membership grew so greatly that a synod with four presbyteries was organized.

---

[1] Approximate membership in the United States: Presbyterian, U.S.A., 2,200,000; Presbyterian U.S., 600,000.

An "Adopting Act" was passed by the general synod, in 1729, by which it was agreed that all ministers of the synod should declare "their agreement in and approbation of the Confession of Faith with the Longer and Shorter Catechisms of the Assembly of Divines at Westminster." For a time (1728 to 1758) there were two parties in the Presbyterian Church: the "Old Side" indorsing the intellectual attitude and the "New Side" indorsing the spiritual attitude. But in 1758 they agreed to adopt the Westminster Standards pure and simple, and were thus united.

During the years 1790 to 1837, the membership increased from 18,000 to 220,500. This was due chiefly to the religious revival which was sweeping the country at that time. Also the plan of co-operation with the Congregational Church, whereby ministers of one church were allowed to serve in the other, greatly added to the strength of this body.

Women have always had a voice in the government of this Church. They vote for pastor and other church officers, and also have their foreign missionary societies and educational work. Each church may also have deaconesses who are under the direction of the session.

The Presbyterian Church has been very loyal to the United States. During World War I it voted at the General Assembly at Dallas, Texas, in 1917, to make to the United States

. . . formal offer of the services of the Presbyterian Church in the United States of America, and upon any request made by the Government, to call upon any or all of the agencies and resources of the Church as in its judgment might be wise or needful.

Commissions were appointed which served the Red Cross and war camps. Its service in World War II was also notable.

WHY?

The Presbyterian churches in America were mostly of English and Scottish origin, although they had no official connection with the churches of the mother country. Their pastors were mostly Church of England ministers who were holding the

Presbyterian views which demanded a spiritually minded ministry and membership. This movement was the result of the influence of Calvin working in the Church of England.

WHAT—IN ORGANIZATION?

The Presbyterian Church has two basic factors: teaching elders or ministers as representatives of Christ, and the ruling elders as representatives of the people. The administrative system is made up of the *session,* which governs the congregation; the *presbytery,* which governs a number of congregations within a limited district; the *synod,* which governs the congregations of a larger district; and the *General Assembly,* which is the supreme judicatory.

The session has charge of the reception of members, discipline, and spiritual affairs of the church.

The presbytery has power "to receive, ordain, install, and judge ministers; to supervise the business which is common to all its congregations; to review session reports; to hear and dispose of cases coming before it on complaint or appeal; and to have oversight of general denominational matters."

The synod has the power "to review the record of its presbyteries, to hear and dispose of all complaints and appeals, to erect new presbyteries, to supervise within the administration of all denominational matters, and, in general, to care for its churches and ministers under the direction of the General Assembly."

The General Assembly. The General Assembly is the highest judiciary of the Church. It is composed of ministers and ruling elders from each presbytery, chosen in the following manner: "Each presbytery consisting of not more than twenty-four ministers shall send one minister and one elder, and each presbytery consisting of more than twenty-four ministers shall send one minister and one elder for each additional twenty-four ministers or for each additional fractional number of ministers not less than twelve."

The duty of the General Assembly is: to decide upon all

controversies concerning doctrine and discipline; to erect new synods, to appoint boards and commissions; to receive and issue all appeals. Its decision is final, except in such cases as affect the constitution of the Church.

Church Membership. All candidates are examined by the session as to their Christian life and belief. An assent to the creed of the Church is not required. Both infants and unbaptized adults are baptized by sprinkling, although in the latter case immersion may be substituted. The Church serves the Lord's Supper to all evangelical Christians. Those who worship regularly but are not members are called "adherents." Only communicants have the rights of full membership.

WHAT—IN BELIEF?

The Presbyterian's standards of belief are the Westminster Confession of Faith and the Larger and Shorter Catechisms. These were adopted in 1729. In 1886 a few alterations were made and a declaratory statement was adopted setting forth "the universality of the gospel offer of salvation, declaring that sinners are condemned only on the ground of their sin, and affirming that all persons dying in infancy are elect and therefore saved."

The fundamental beliefs[2] of the Presbyterian Church, based on Calvinism, are as follows:

1. The sovereignty of God in Christ in the salvation of the individual.
2. Each believer's salvation is a part of an eternal divine plan.
3. Salvation is a spiritual gift from God and is not a reward for faith.
4. Man is utterly unable to save himself.
5. Regeneration is an act of God alone.

---

[2] ". . . most of the Presbyterian Churches adhere, with greater or less strictness, to the system of doctrine developed by John Calvin, in which the sovereignty and supreme will of God receive chief emphasis. Recent generations of Presbyterians have been interpreting this truth in terms of God's loving will."—LOETSCHER

6. Those who are once actually saved will always remain saved.

While the Church insists upon the supreme importance of the spiritual life, it gives both the minister and the laity full liberty to worship God as their consciences direct. The Presbyterians have stressed education and maintain a very high standard for the ordination to the Christian ministry. They also specialize in good preaching.[3]

HELPS FOR STUDY

Written Work

1. When and where was the Presbyterian Church established in America?
2. Why do we have a Presbyterian Church in this country?
3. What do the following terms mean: session, presbytery, synod, General Assembly?
4. What does this Church believe?

Oral Discussion

1. Why may this Church be called "the Church of doctrine"?
2. How do the Protestant Episcopal and the Presbyterian denominations differ?
3. What is the difference between the Presbyterian Church, U.S.A. and the Presbyterian Church, U.S.?
4. What has the Presbyterian Church U.S.A. done for relief and reconstruction?
5. For what purposes did this denomination raise its Restoration Fund?

Special Assignments

1. Look up the present standing of this Church.
2. Outline Chapter VII of Brown's *The Larger Faith*.
3. Indicate how the Presbyterian type of government is constituted like that of a republic.
4. Show how a confession of faith can be modernized.

---

[3] See *A Brief History of the Presbyterians*, by Lefferts A. Loetscher (Board of Christian Education, Presbyterian Church, U.S.A., Philadelphia, Pennsylvania). This book contains a valuable bibliography.

THE CHURCH OF VISION
. . . the Congregational Christian Churches[1]

For rigorous teachers seized my youth,
And purged its faith, and trimm'd its fire,
Show'd me the high, white star of Truth,
There bade me gaze, and there aspire.

MATTHEW ARNOLD

WHEN AND WHERE?

It was Robert Browne, a pastor holding the Separatists' position, who founded the Congregational Church in England. In 1581 he, with his congregation, emigrated to Holland because of the persecutions which were being directed against all Separatists. But the movement could not be killed, and in 1604 John Robinson, a pastor of a congregation at Scrooby, accepted the beliefs of Browne. This meant exile for him and so he and a number of friends went to Amsterdam, and then to Leyden. At both of these places they met with a friendly reception, but wishing to rear their children as Englishmen they decided to settle in America. This Pilgrim band, one hundred and two strong, under the leadership of Brewster, Bradford, and Winslow landed upon the shores of Plymouth, Mass., in 1620. Here they founded the first Congregational church upon American soil. A few years later the Puritans of Massachusetts

---

[1] Approximately 1,200,000 members in the United States.

Bay combined with the Pilgrims, thus forming a strong alliance. By 1640 there were thirty-one Congregational Churches in New England and as a result of this rapid growth Congregationalism became practically a state religion. But with the beginning of the eighteenth century such bodies as the Baptists and Quakers protested against being taxed for the support of the Congregational Church. This protest ended the experiment of a State-Church in America.

This Church took the initiative in the revival known as the "Great Awakening," which began in 1734. It also played an important part in the political discussions which preceded the Revolutionary War, sending such men as John Hancock and the Adamses to take part in the councils.

During the century succeeding the Revolutionary War the history of this Church centers about the following movements: a plan of union with the Presbyterian Church; the development of missionary enterprise; the Unitarian separation; the extension of the denomination in the West; the organization of a National Council; an attempt to secure a uniform statement of Congregational belief.

The Congregational Church has always put great stress on missions, both at home and on the foreign field. It has done pioneer work through the American Board of Commissioners for Foreign Missions (1810) and the American Home Missionary Society (1826), which, in 1861, became the Congregational Home Missionary Society. It has also taken a very prominent part in the Federal Council of the Churches of Christ in America and has cooperated heartily in all movements to promote the Christian life in church and country.

In 1931 it merged with the Christian denomination, taking the name of "Congregational Christian Churches." A union with the Evangelical and Reformed Church has been under serious discussion.

WHY?

The Congregational Church is a development of the Separatists of England. This body believed that it should not remain within the established church, for it maintained that the whole system of the Establishment was far from the Christian ideal and merely a shallow imitation of the true Church. Believing that it could not be reformed, they, as true Christians, withdrew from it.

WHAT—IN ORGANIZATION?

The local church is the center and unit of Congregationalism. Each member, irrespective of sex or position, has an equal vote in its management. The officers of the church are the pastor, a board of deacons, a clerk and treasurer, a board of trustees, and heads of various committees of church work. These have no ecclesiastical authority but are set apart for these special services.

For mutual help, the churches gather in local conferences, state conferences, and the National Council. Membership in the National Council includes ministerial and lay delegates elected by the state and district conferences. Neither these conferences nor the National Council have ecclesiastical authority.

Ordination to the ministry takes place either in the candidate's home church or in the church where he is to be installed as pastor, before a council of churches. Here practical Christian fellowship is emphasized more than mere doctrinal tests. The ordained pastor has no ecclesiastical authority. He becomes a member of the church which he serves.

Admission to church membership is on the declared purpose to lead a Christian life, rather than on the acceptance of any creed. Participation in the Lord's Supper is free to all who profess to follow Christ. The form of baptism is optional, although sprinkling is customary.

WHAT—IN BELIEF?

Although the denomination, as a body, has no creed, yet the local churches have the right to frame their own statement of doctrinal belief. There have been several attempts to draw up a consensus of belief for all the churches. The first of these attempts was the "Cambridge Platform," which simply registered the general approval of the Westminster Confession. But this was not accepted by all the churches and another attempt was made in the "Savoy Confession" (1680), but this was too much like the former and was not fully accepted. In 1880, the National Council appointed a commission to prepare "a formula that shall not be mainly a reaffirmation of former confessions, but that shall state in precise terms in our living tongue the doctrines that we hold today." The statement which was issued was never formally adopted, yet it served as the doctrinal basis for the majority of the churches.[2]

In 1913, as the result of an appeal for a more definite platform of belief, the National Council adopted the following statement, which has been accepted with practical unanimity by the denomination:

Preamble. The Congregational Churches of the United States, by delegates in the National Council assembled, reserving all the rights and cherished memories belonging to this organization under its former constitution, and declaring the steadfast allegiance of the churches composing the Council to the faith which our fathers confessed, which from age to age has found expression in the historic creeds of the Church universal and of this communion, and affirming our loyalty to the basic principles of our representative democracy, hereby set forth the things most surely believed among us concerning faith, polity, and fellowship.

Faith. We believe in God, the Father, infinite in wisdom, goodness and love; and in Jesus Christ, His Son, our Lord and Saviour, who for us and our salvation lived and died, and rose again and liveth evermore; and in the Holy Spirit, who taketh of the things of Christ and revealeth them to us, renewing, comforting, and inspiring the souls of men. We are united in striving to know the will of God, as taught in the Holy Scriptures, and our purpose to walk in the ways of the Lord, made known or to be made known to us. We hold it to be the mission of the Church of Christ to proclaim the gospel to all mankind, exalting the worship of the true God, and laboring for the progress of knowledge, the promotion of justice,

---

[2] See *History of American Congregationalism*, by Gaius Glenn Atkins and Frederick L. Fagley (Pilgrim Press, Boston, Massachusetts).

the reign of peace, and the realization of human brotherhood. Depending, as did our fathers, upon the continued guidance of the Holy Spirit to lead us into all truth, we work and pray for the transformation of the world into the Kingdom of God; and we look with faith for the triumph of righteousness and the life everlasting.

Polity. We believe in the freedom and responsibility of the individual soul and the right of private judgment. We hold to the autonomy of the local church and its independence of all ecclesiastical control. We cherish the fellowship of the churches united in district, states, and national bodies, for counsel and cooperation in matters of common concern.

The Wider Fellowship. While affirming the liberty of our churches, and the validity of our ministry, we hold to the unity and catholicity of the church of Christ, and will unite with all its branches in hearty cooperation; and will earnestly seek, so far as in us lies, that the prayer of our Lord may be answered, that they all may be one.[3]

HELPS FOR STUDY

Written Work

1. Give the history of the Congregational Christian Churches.
2. Why does the Congregational Church exist?
3. What type of organization has it?
4. Make a summary of its beliefs.

Oral Discussion

1. Why may this Church be called "the teaching Church"?
2. Is democracy always the best form of government?
3. How much of a distinction is made between minister and congregation?
4. Why can a person believe in science and religion at the same time?
5. What part have denominations played in the founding of schools and colleges in this country?

---

[3] See *An Adventure in Liberty, A Short History of the Congregational Christian Churches* (The Missionary Herald, New York City).

Special Assignments

1. Look up the biographies of the following men: Henry Ward Beecher, Lyman Abbott, George A. Gordon, and S. Parkes Cadman.

2. Outline Chapter II of Brown's *The Larger Faith*.

3. Show that Congregationalists have been the pioneers in education and missions.

4. Show how the Congregational Christian Churches have contributed to freedom and individualism in religion.

5. Discover the relationship of the Congregational Christian Churches to the Evangelical and Reformed Church.

·23·

THE CHURCH OF FAITH
. . . the Lutheran Church[1]

> From heart to heart, from creed to creed,
>   The hidden river runs;
> It quickens all the ages down,
>   It binds the sires to sons,—
> The stream of Faith, whose source is God,
>   Whose sound, the sound of prayer,
> Whose meadows are the holy lives
>   Upspringing everywhere.

WILLIAM CHANNING GANNETT

WHEN AND WHERE?

The first Lutherans to settle in North America came from
Holland to Manhattan Island in 1623. For many years they
were not allowed to establish their own form of worship, for the
authorities had received instructions "to encourage no other
doctrine in the New Netherland than the true Reformed." But
in 1674 the English took possession of New York and the
Lutherans were granted full liberty.

The first independent colony of Lutherans was established in
1638 on the Delaware River by some Swedes sent over by the
prime minister of King Adolphus. Reorus Torkillus was the first
Lutheran minister to settle in the United States. This was in

---

[1] Approximate membership in the United States: United Lutheran
Church of America, 1,800,000; Evangelical Lutheran Synod of Missouri,
Ohio, and other states, 1,500,000; Evangelical Lutheran Church, 662,000;
Augustana Synod, 400,000; American Lutheran Church, 602,000.

1639. Soon afterward a church was built at Fort Christina, where he held services.

Other churches were established by Swedish and German immigrants in Pennsylvania, Delaware, Virginia, the Carolinas, and Georgia. By the middle of the eighteenth century Pennsylvania alone contained about thirty thousand Lutherans. The first synod, that of Pennsylvania, was organized by Muhlenberg (a man who took for his motto, "Ecclesia Plantand"), patriarch of the Lutheran Church in America, in 1748. The second synod, that of New York, was formed in 1786. By 1818, the growth of the denomination had become very rapid. In 1820, the General Synod was formed, mostly through the work of Schmucker, founder of the Gettysburg Theological Seminary.

This growth was due mostly to immigration from such Lutheran countries as Sweden, Norway, Denmark, Finland, and Germany. The larger proportion was composed of Germans. In 1918 nearly all of the different factors of the body united to form the United Lutheran Church in America, the most notable exception being the Augustana Synod and the Missouri Synod.

Today the communicants of the Lutheran bodies in the United States number about five million members. Throughout the world "Lutheranism represents about 47 per cent of Protestantism, and 5 per cent of the world population." It is now the established church in Denmark, Norway, and Sweden, and most of the Protestant population of the German states belong to this body. In fact this Church is well represented in practically every country around the Baltic.

WHY?

The Lutheran Church dates from the time of the Reformation. It can be said without causing too much opposition that Martin Luther was responsible for its origin. Although he had no intention of forming a denomination, the faith which bears his name has spread to the uttermost bounds of the earth in the form of the Lutheran churches. Therefore the spirit of the Protestant Reformation—that of dissatisfaction with the Roman Catholic Church and a strong belief in salvation by faith in

Christ—still lives in the world in the form of the ever zealous Lutheran Church.

WHAT—IN ORGANIZATION?

For the most part the Lutheran Church is congregational in polity, especially when the authority of ecclesiastical bodies over the local churches is concerned, but for general administrative and consultative purposes it is representative.

The organization of the local church is composed of the congregation and a church council made up of the pastor and the church officers. The church officers are composed of elders and deacons, and sometimes trustees. When there are no trustees, the deacons take care of the temporal affairs of the church. Each church governs its own affairs according to its constitution.

Besides the local churches, there are conferences and synods. These vary in constitution and in form. Some have no ecclesiastical authority, while others have committed to them legislative authority and their action is recognized by the churches. But for the most part the local church has the right to voice its approval or disapproval in these matters and to keep or drop its pastor from the rolls of the church.

The Lutheran Church has a liturgical form of worship and observes the various general festivals of the Christian Church. Archbishop Nathan Söderblom of Upsala, has said in regard to this:

Beside the pulpit which unites us with our brethren in Evangelic Christendom, we have in our sanctuaries an altar, which unites us *mutatis mutandis* with our brethren in Orthodox and Roman Christendom. (Both pulpit and altar are found also in Anglicanism). The altar means adoration and mystery. The altar and the sacrament of the altar mean that human understanding is unable to grasp the mystery of salvation. There is a place in our common worship as well as in theology, where reason recognizes its inability and falls down in adoration. No sect in Western Christendom outside the Church of Rome has accentuated in its doctrine the Real Presence and the mysterious communion of the sacrament as has our Evangelic Lutheran sect, although our faith repudiates any quasi-rational magical explanation of the virtue of the sacrament.

WHAT—IN BELIEF?

As it has already been said: know Martin Luther's beliefs, and you will know the doctrines of the Lutheran Church. In Chapter XV, page 110, you will find Martin Luther's chief beliefs. In brief, these are the main convictions held by the Lutheran Church:

1. Justification is by faith alone.
2. The word of God is the only rule and source of faith.
3. The Lord's Supper is more than a memorial; it is a channel of God's grace.
4. Baptism affords the potential gift of regeneration from the Holy Spirit.
5. Infant baptism is regarded as proper and fitting.

The whole doctrine of this Church centers in the gospel of Christ for the fallen man. This is summed up in the Augsburg Confession. Dean Brown says in regard to this Church:

The Lutheran Church is a liturgical church and it exalts the value of the sacraments. But it does not allow "the outward and visible sign of an inward and spiritual grace" to interpose itself in any mechanical way between the heart of the communicant and the Real Presence of the Spirit of Christ abiding within the soul of the believer. "The sole value of the sacrament," Luther taught, "is its witness to the divine promise. It strengthens faith. It seals or attests the God-given pledge of union with Christ and the forgiveness of sins."

HELPS FOR STUDY

Written Work

1. When and where was the Lutheran Church established in America?
2. Why do we have a Lutheran Church in history?
3. What type of organization has this Church?
4. Give the doctrines of this denomination.

Oral Discussion

1. What happened to the Lutheran Church in Germany during World War II?

2. How does the National Lutheran Council serve its constituent members?

3. What is the real strength of Lutheranism?

4. In what ways have Lutherans aided their brethren in Europe during the post-war years?

Special Assignments

1. Outline Chapter V of Brown's *The Larger Faith*.

2. Write an essay on the use of faith in everyday life.

3. Play and sing the Lutheran hymn, "A Mighty Fortress Is Our God."

4. Comment on this statement:

The power of Lutheranism to conserve the theology of the sixteenth century in the midst of a modern world has been equaled by its love of religious liberty and political independence.

THE CHURCH OF CONCERN
. . . the Reformed Church[1]

O purblind race of miserable men,
How many among us even at this hour
Do forge a lifelong trouble for ourselves
By taking true for false, or false for true?

                                        TENNYSON

WHEN AND WHERE?

Many were the sects which sprang up as a result of the
Protestant Reformation. Those sects which cannot trace their
origin back to Luther can usually trace it back to Zwingli,
Calvin, and Melancthon. Of those which fall in the latter class
there are: the Reformed Church of Switzerland, Holland, and
Germany; the Presbyterian Church of Scotland and England;
the Huguenot Church of France; and the national churches of
Bohemia and Hungary. All of these represent nearly the same
general movement.

When the Dutch and the Germans emigrated to America they
brought the Reformed Church along with them. The first Reformed Church in America was that on Manhattan Island, which
was organized by the Dutch, in 1628. Later some Germans,
being driven from the Palatinate by the severe persecutions of
Louis XIV, settled in upper New York and Pennsylvania. As
immigration increased the Dutch made their headquarters in

---

[1] Approximate membership in the United States: Reformed in America,
177,000 members; Christian Reformed, 135,000 members.

Michigan, where they could cooperate with the New York branch, which came to be known as "The Reformed Church in America." The German Reformed Church became "The Reformed Church in the United States."

At first these bodies held to their own language and customs. This, of course, checked the natural growth, and the practice was abandoned. Now the use of English has been accepted and this Church has become, to a great extent, Americanized. This body remains conservative, however. Yet it is a friendly Church and enters gladly into interdenominational relations. It has always had a missionary outlook and stands for the best in education and scholarship.

WHY?

What Martin Luther is to the Lutheran Church, so Zwingli and Calvin are to the Reformed Church. It had its beginning in Switzerland in 1516. Although it is contemporary with the Lutheran Church, it has no official connection with it. After the early death of Zwingli, John Calvin became the leader of this body. Because of Calvin's influence, it holds a very distinct type of Calvinistic doctrine and a Presbyterian polity (see Zwingli's views in Chapter XV).

WHAT—IN ORGANIZATION?

The Reformed Church has a presbyterian type of organization. That is, the local church is controlled by a consistory which is composed of ministers, elders, and deacons who are elected by the members of the church. The ministers and elders attend to the spiritual affairs while the deacons care for the secular matters.

The local church organization differs from the Presbyterian system in that the elders and deacons, the consistory, are the trustees.

The Reformed Church in America is governed by a General Synod which meets annually and has the following organizations: Board of Directors, Board of Domestic Missions (Church Building Fund), Women's Board of Domestic Missions, Board of Foreign Missions, Board of Education, Young People's Work, The Minister's Fund, and the United Advance Fund. It has many of the most historic colonial churches of New York and New Jersey. Today it has many strong churches in the Middle and Far West.

WHAT—IN BELIEF?

The doctrine of the Reformed Church is represented in the Apostles', the Nicene, and the Athanasian creeds. Also the Canons of the Synod of Dort, the Belgic Confession, and the Heidelberg Catechism all contain statements of their belief. It is distinctly a Calvinistic body. Stress is placed upon liturgy.

Children are baptized "as heirs of the kingdom of God and of his covenant," while adults are baptized on profession of faith in Christ unto the remission of sins.

The church membership consists of all baptized persons. These are under the care of the Church, and are subject to its government and discipline. The prospective members do not sign any specific creed, but they are required to make a confession of faith before the minister and elders.

The Lord's Supper is practiced, with emphasis placed upon the spiritual presence of Christ at the Supper. Here is one of the chief differences between the Lutheran and the Reformed churches. The Reformed Church also has more of a sense of mission and a devotion to the expression of Christianity in the community.

HELPS FOR STUDY

Written Work

1. Give the history of the Reformed Church in America.
2. What relation has this Church with Zwingli?
3. Describe the organization of this Church.
4. What creeds represent the beliefs of the Reformed Church?

Oral Discussion

1. What has John Calvin left to the world as his special contribution?

2. Have Christian missions a great future?

3. How can Protestantism make an impact upon modern civilization?

4. Is Communism a mortal enemy of Christianity?

5. What must the Christian Church do in order to be saved?

Special Assignments

1. Look up the numerical standing of the Reformed Church.

2. List some of the missionaries and mission fields of this denomination.

3. Write a brief account of the life of Zwingli.

· 25 ·

THE CHURCH OF FREEDOM
. . . the Baptist Churches[1]

Let Cæsar's dues be ever paid
To Cæsar and his throne;
But conscience and the soul were made
To be the Lord's alone.

WATTS

WHEN AND WHERE?

There are some who say that the Baptist churches had their origin in the Apostolic Age. It has been said that:

Baptists began with the churches of the New Testament. They are not Protestants. They flourished down to the uniting of the Church and the State by the Emperor Constantine and continued through the Middle Ages in the secluded parts of Europe. They existed under various names, always, however, maintaining certain Baptist characteristics.

This statement may be true in a vague sense of the Baptists, but it is also true of many other denominations as well. It is certain that a line of Baptist churches cannot be traced back to the Apostolic Church. The Baptist churches and Baptist principles are two different things.

The Baptist churches, as we know them today, are purely an English product. The first church of this denomination was established by a body of English refugees who settled in Amster-

---

[1] Approximate membership in the United States: Northern Baptists, 1,600,000; Southern Baptists, 6,080,000; Negro Baptists, 6,700,000.

dam, Holland, in 1608. They were closely connected with the Congregationalists, led by Robinson and Smyth, in Holland. It was this John Smyth who established the church in Amsterdam. In 1611, Thomas Helwys returned to England with part of Smyth's congregation because they were unwilling to be united with the Mennonite Church as Smyth desired. They established the first Baptist church in England at London during the same year (1611).

There is a question in regard to the establishment of the first Baptist church in America. The honor very probably falls upon the church at Providence, Rhode Island, established by Roger Williams, in 1639, although the First Baptist Church of Newport, Rhode Island, claims this title, being founded in the same year by John Clarke. (We had better let the two churches settle this point for themselves.) But we may say that it was Roger Williams, the "Apostle of Religious Liberty," who was the founder and, for a while, leader of the Baptist movement in America.

There have been divisions in this denomination, such as: the Primitive, United, General, Free, etc. The largest body is now known simply as the "Baptists." This body, however, includes the Northern, Southern, and Colored Conventions. The divisions are largely for administrative purposes and imply no marked divergence either in doctrine or ecclesiastical order. When the strength of the Baptists is to be considered, all of these bodies should be included. The Baptists of the whole world, numbering some fourteen million, are united in the Baptist World Alliance.

There has been a very marked advance in the missionary activities, both home and foreign, during recent years.

WHY?

The Baptist churches are founded upon two great principles: personal liberty and freedom of belief. Smyth refused to accept infant baptism for the simple reason that it was in direct opposition to these beliefs. In the same way, Roger Williams refused to bow either before State or Church, and in so doing established a body of followers who recognized the Scriptures as their only rule of guidance and discipline.

WHAT—IN ORGANIZATION?

The Baptist churches have an independent and congregational form of organization. Each church is a separate unit, having control over its own worship and discipline, the calling and dismissal of the pastor, the election of all church officers, deacons and trustees.

A candidate for church membership is usually examined by a body of deacons in regard to his Christian experience and then voted upon by the members of the church. Admission to membership is preceded by baptism by immersion, although in some Baptist churches members from other churches are received who have not been immersed. This is on the basis of an associate membership. The new member is required to sign no creed, but only to accept the New Testament as the sole guide in the religious life.

The officers of the church consist of: the pastor, deacons, trustees, treasurer and clerk, and sometimes a standing (or advisory) committee which is composed of the pastor and officials with several other members elected by the church. This committee has no authority except that granted by the members. The church property is generally held by a board of trustees, or it may be held either under the control of the entire society or of a special committee.

Ministers are licensed to preach by the church where they hold their membership. When ordination is desired, the candidate is brought before a council, called by the candidate's church, which is composed of selected members of sister churches. Here the candidate is questioned in regard to his religious experience, his call to the ministry, and his views on certain doctrines. When the candidate becomes a pastor he becomes a member of the church which he serves. He has no special authority and is under the discipline of the church which he is serving.

The churches unite in associations where reports from the various churches are read and recommendations are made. These associations have no authority and meet merely for mutual help. Besides these area associations there are state conventions, City Mission Societies, and various national missionary, educational, and pension boards. A national convention, which meets annually, is the top organization. These conventions of Northern, Southern, and National (colored) Baptists have no authority over the individual churches, boards, or societies.

WHAT—IN BELIEF?

Baptists have no creed; neither do they have any imposed statements of faith. As Dr. E. Y. Mullins has said:

No central authority speaks for Baptists. Their church and district associations usually announce certain cardinal truths of Christianity in order to define themselves. But these are never imposed upon others. They are merely testimonies to the way in which the Bible is understood and interpreted. They are not identical in meaning, although there has been remarkable unity among Baptists.

The two principal confessions are the Philadelphia Confession (1689) and the New Hampshire Confession (1832). Neither of these is a true statement of Baptist beliefs, nor in any way binding. All the Baptists are free to interpret the Scriptures as the conscience directs, and a wide margin is set in which beliefs may be modified as new light comes through science and education. It is impossible, therefore, to define Baptist churches in so many words, because each church and each member is given the privilege to worship God through Jesus Christ with an open mind and a spiritual outlook.

The great truths which Baptists hold can be summed up as follows:

1. That each church should be independent.
2. That there should be entire separation of Church and State.
3. That there should be religious liberty in all matters of belief.
4. That the Church is composed of regenerated people who are followers of the Christ.

5. That infant baptism is un-Scriptural and should not be practiced.

6. That only believers should be baptized, for the form has no power of salvation in itself. The only correct practice is immersion.

7. That the Lord's Supper should be observed as a memorial of Jesus Christ.

8. That the Bible is the Word of God and should be interpreted according to the best judgment of each individual.

Baptists maintain a Joint Conference Committee on Public Relations, with an office in Washington, D. C., mostly for the purpose of making known on a national level their convictions concerning the separation of Church and State. At the Baptist World Congress, held in Copenhagen, Denmark, in the summer of 1947, they adopted a "Manifesto on Religious Freedom," which says in part:

Holding the principles of freedom dear, we therefore seek for all peoples everywhere, and in particular for all minority groups the following freedoms:

Freedom to determine their own faith and beliefs;

Freedom of public and private worship, preaching and teaching;

Freedom from any opposition by the State of religious ceremonies and forms of worship;

Freedom to determine the nature of their own ecclesiastical government and the qualifications of their ministers and members, including the right of the individual to join the church of his own choice, and the right to associate for cooperative Christian action;

Freedom to control the education of their ministers, to give religious instruction to their youth, and to provide for the adequate development of their own religious life;

Freedom of Christian service, relief work and missionary activity, both at home and abroad; and

Freedom to own and use such facilities and properties as will make possible the accomplishment of these ends.

HELPS FOR STUDY

Written Work

1. Give the history of the Baptists.
2. Upon what two principles are the Baptist churches founded?
3. What type of organization have they?
4. Give a summary of the beliefs of the Baptists.

Oral Discussion

1. Are the Baptist churches really churches of freedom?
2. Do organizations always live up to their ideals?
3. What are the "Fundamentalists" up to within the Northern Baptist Convention?
4. Why do the Southern Baptists refuse to join the World Council of Churches?
5. What is the value of infant baptism?
6. Must one be baptized in order to be a Christian?

Special Assignments

1. Compare the strength of the Methodists and the Baptists.
2. Outline Chapter I of Brown's *The Larger Faith*.
3. Play and sing the Baptist hymn, "He Leadeth Me."
4. Give a summary of the Westminster Confession.
5. Show how the Baptists have contributed to the simple forms of faith.
6. Make a study of Jesus' attitude toward baptism.

· 26 ·

THE CHURCH OF LIGHT
. . . the Quakers[1]

Our Friend, our Brother, and our Lord,
What may Thy service be?
Nor name, nor form, nor ritual word,
But simply following Thee.

WHITTIER

WHEN AND WHERE?

George Fox, the founder of this "denomination," was born in 1624, at Leicestershire, England. His religious experience is told in Chapter XVII. The teaching which he emphasized—that of direct communication with God and the abolishment of all forms and creeds—was something new for his day. But soon he gathered a band of preachers who went all through England and Ireland teaching about the "inner light." They had no intention of establishing a new sect, but merely to win people to a more spiritual life. However, as their number increased a loose organization was formed, called "The Children of Light." Later they called themselves the "Religious Society of Friends," and were commonly called "Quakers."

These Friends were severely persecuted in England, chiefly because they refused to attend the services of the Established Church, to pay tithes, to take oaths, or to fight in war. Many of these were fined, and not a few were cast into the jails; yet

---

[1] Approximate membership of various bodies of Friends in the United States, 114,000.

persecution did not put out the "inner light" of these friendly people. On the contrary, Rountree reports that:

During the Commonwealth, and throughout the reign of Charles II, the Friends were constantly growing in number in England and in other countries, and by 1690 were a numerous as well as a well-organized people.

The first Friends, or Quakers, to arrive in this country (Massachusetts) were Ann Austin and Mary Fisher (1656), but they were taken for witches and sent back to Barbados whence they came. For many years severe laws were put upon the Quakers and they were treated without mercy. However they began to increase in America, and at last found a welcome in Rhode Island. They were also to be found in New York, New Jersey, and Maryland; but the far greater number settled in Pennsylvania under William Penn.

Why?

The Society of Friends is the result of a yearning in the hearts of many English people for a more spiritual type of Christianity. These people protested against all ecclesiasticism, sacramentarianism, and traditionalism, and demanded a more ethical and practical religion. As Rountree states, it was their hope that:

. . . all Christian people might come to obey the light of Christ in their own hearts, and that so great a reformation, social as well as religious, might be wrought through Christendom.

These Seekers found in George Fox a trusty leader, and under his guidance have given the modern world a demonstration of true religion such as Jesus had.

What—in Organization?

The worship of the Friends is based upon three verses of Scripture: First, "God is a Spirit, and they that worship Him must worship in spirit and in truth" (John 4:24); second, "Where the Spirit of the Lord is, there is liberty" (2 Corinthians

3: 17) ; and third, "Let all things be done decently and in order" (1 Corinthians 14: 40). Therefore, they meet in silence at a stated hour, they have no sacred building, and all are free to take part in the meeting if they are so led by the "inner light."

They do have "church" officers—elders and ministers—who are selected by the members because of their special calling. It is the duty of the elders to have charge of the conduct of the public worship, while the minister cares for the spiritual matters. There is, however, no line of distinction drawn between the laity and the clergy, for they hold that all Christians are ministers or priests. When a member has especial ability to speak and to give spiritual help he is usually recommended for the ministry (women may become ministers as well as men). They usually receive no salary and continue to work at the ordinary tasks at which they were formerly engaged. There are a few who form a separate class, however, such as those occupied with full-time religious service at home and abroad. These have their living expenses paid by the Society. On the whole the Friends do not approve of giving or receiving money for gospel service.

The Society is governed by a series of meetings: preparative (congregational), monthly, quarterly, and yearly. In these meetings any member of the Society is free to take part. There is no voting, but decisions are arrived at through the "sense of the meeting." When a diversity of opinion is felt by the clerk of the meeting, the assembly is adjourned until some later date.

The business of the monthly meeting is to receive and exclude members, to care for the poor and the education of children, to appoint church officers, to liberate ministers for religious service, to appoint registering officers, overseers, and elders.

The quarterly meeting is composed of all the monthly meetings within a certain district and its business is partly devotional and partly executive. The yearly meeting is the unit of authority, and every member of the Society belongs to this body and all are equally free to speak.

Marriage, to the Friends, is a religious ordinance as well as a civil contract. Therefore, when a couple desires to get married, they merely go before a meeting and mutually promise to be faithful to each other as husband and wife. Thus they are wed.

What—in Belief?

The Friends have no creeds nor sacraments. They will not take oaths; neither will they fight. They dress simply and talk plainly. It is their purpose to cultivate the "inner light" and to make God a vital experience.

They believe supremely in the nearness of God to the human soul, in direct intercourse and immediate communion, in mystical experience in a first-hand discovery of God. . . . It means and involves a sensitiveness to the wider spiritual Life above us, around us, and within us, a dedication to duty, a passion for truth, and an appreciation for goodness, an eagerness to let love and the grace of God come freely through one's own life, a reverence for the will of God wherever it is revealed in past or present, and a high faith that Christ is a living presence and a life-giving energy always within reach of the receptive soul.—RUFUS JONES.

The doctrines of the Quakers agree in all essential points with the other Protestant denominations, but they differ in such matters as:

1. The emphasis placed upon the "inner light."
2. The absence of all form, including baptism and the Lord's Supper.
3. The belief that all Christians are "priests."
4. Their manner of worship and the appointment of ministers.
5. The doctrine of non-resistance.
6. The belief that the baptism of the Spirit and the fellowship with the Father and Son fulfill all spiritual obligations.
7. The refusal to take oaths.
8. No special training given to the ministry.
9. That marriage is an act of God, and therefore cannot be performed but only witnessed by man.
10. The emphasis placed upon sincerity, both in word and deed.

HELPS FOR STUDY

Written Work

1. Who was George Fox and what did he do?
2. How were the early Friends treated in America?
3. What caused the Friends to organize?
4. What kind of an organization do they have?
5. What special beliefs do they hold?

Oral Discussion

1. Why did the Society of Friends receive the Nobel Peace Prize?
2. Is non-resistance a sensible policy?
3. What are some of the greatest contributions made by Quakers to America?
4. Is preaching too much of a profession today?
5. What part should silence play in worship?

Special Assignments

1. Look up the biography of Rufus Jones.
2. Study some of the poems of Whittier.
3. Write an essay on friendship.
4. Find the author to the words of the Friend's hymn, "Immortal Love Forever Full, Forever Flowing Free."
5. Look up something about John Woolman, Joseph Sturge, and John Bright.
6. Show the progress that has been made in the attempt to abolish war.

27

THE CHURCH OF ACTION
. . . *The Methodist Church*[1]

> *Thou, O Christ, art all I want;*
> *More than all in Thee I find:*
> *Raise the fallen, cheer the faint,*
> *Heal the sick, and lead the blind.*
> *Just and holy is Thy name;*
> *I am all unrighteousness;*
> *False and full of sin I am,*
> *Thou art full of truth and grace.*
>
> CHARLES WESLEY (1740)

WHEN AND WHERE?

The Methodist Church, both in Europe and America, was the outcome of a movement begun at Oxford University, in 1729, by John and Charles Wesley and George Whitefield. These men and their followers believed that no person could be saved without holiness, and thus they were first named "the Holy Club." It should be noted that this body was a part of the Church of England, and at no time did the Wesleys break their ministerial relations with the Church. But the Church of England objected to the doctrine and practice of these people and soon the leaders of this little band found themselves excluded

---

[1] Approximate membership of The Methodist Church in the United States, 8,500,000; Africa M. E., 870,000; African M. E. Zion, 490,000; Colored Methodist Episcopal, 381,000.

from many of the pulpits of the Established Church. For this reason they were compelled to hold their services in private houses, halls, and barns, and many times out of doors. As their numbers grew, societies for worship were formed and out of these grew the class meetings, lay preachers, and the itineracy. The complete organization was accomplished in 1744, when the Wesleys met their workers in the first annual conference. But it was not until 1795 that they separated from the Anglican Church.

The first group of Methodists to come to America was in 1760, when Philip Embury, a Wesleyan preacher from Ireland, landed in New York with his Irish class. In 1768 they dedicated a chapel which has come to be known as "John Street Church." After this other preachers, including Francis Asbury, were sent over by John Wesley, and in 1784 they met in their first conference at Baltimore.

As a result of the Revolutionary War, The Methodist Church in America broke all connection with the mother country. John Wesley wrote:

Our American brothers are now totally disentangled both from the State and the English hierarchy. We dare not entangle them again, either with the one or with the other. They are now at full liberty to follow the Scriptures and the primitive Church.

The first General Conference was held in 1792. In 1800 Richard Whatcoat was elected bishop, and in 1808 William McKendree was elected to that office. He was the first native American to hold this position. The first Methodist Sunday School in America was established in 1786, in Hanover County, Va., the Missionary Society was formed in 1819, the Sunday School Union in 1827, the Board of Education in 1868, the Women's Foreign Missionary Society in 1869, and the Epworth League in 1889.

The Uniting Conference of April, 1939, which formed The Methodist Church, brought into one great denomination The Methodist Episcopal Church, The Methodist Episcopal Church South, and The Methodist Protestant Church.

WHY?

As Emerson says:

An institution is the lengthened shadow of one man: as monarch-ism, of the Hermit Anthony; the Reformation, of Luther; Quaker-ism of Fox; Methodism of Wesley; abolition, of Clarkson.

In the case of this denomination, John Wesley is its founder. To appreciate the bigness of this man, we have only to look at his weekly schedule while at Oxford (as given by himself): Mondays and Tuesdays devoted to Greek and Roman classics, historians, and poets; Wednesday to logic and ethics; Thursdays to Hebrew and Arabic; Fridays to metaphysics and natural philosophy; Saturdays to oratory and poetry, chiefly compos-ing; Sundays to divinity.

This scholar, along with his brother Charles, formed a club at Oxford (November, 1729) for the purpose of living, as Wesley puts it, "by rule and method." Because of their order and system they earned for themselves the name "Methodists." These men believed in primitive Christian doctrine and pos-sessed a theology which was experimental and evangelical. They stressed the renewal and sanctification of each individual through faith in Jesus Christ. John Wesley expresses this belief when he testifies:

I felt my heart strangely warmed, I felt I did trust in Christ, Christ alone for salvation; and an assurance was given me that he had taken away my sins, even mine, and saved me from the law of sin and death.

As these doctrines were not held by the Church of England those who held them were expelled from the Church.

But the Church of England, during this period, knew no better than to do this. It had lost its way, its theology was cold, its clergy was for the most part ignorant and unspiritual, and its services were all form. Wesley and his followers desired to bring the Church back to a spiritual foundation. They went forth preaching repentance and salvation, until all England was on fire with a new spirit. This was the birth of one of the largest Protestant denominations in the world.

WHAT—IN ORGANIZATION?

The organization of The Methodist Church consists of the local church, the ministry, and a system of conferences.

Church Membership. The membership is of two classes: full members and preparatory members. The preparatory relation is required before coming into full membership. These members have all church privileges except voting or being voted for. When the required period (indefinite time) is over and the candidate has passed through the classes of preparation, the person is received into full membership on recommendation of the official board.

Full members (both sexes) vote in all church matters and are eligible to all local church offices and to membership in all the conferences, except the annual.

Church Officers. These consist of the pastor, class leaders, stewards, trustees, superintendents of Sunday Schools, and presidents of societies.

Pastors are appointed by the bishop at the annual conference.

Class leaders are appointed by the pastor.

Local preachers are licensed by the quarterly conference.

Other officers are elected by the various departments and are confirmed by the quarterly conference.

There is a class of lay preachers, which is granted licenses to preach by the district or quarterly conference. These usually do not give up their ordinary business.

Church Finance. Each Methodist church is practically independent in regard to its own financial affairs. However, it is under the general ecclesiastical system. The salary of the pastor of a local church is fixed by an estimating committee of the quarterly conferences in which he serves.

Bishops. They are elders who are elected by the general conference and consecrated by three bishops, or by one bishop and two elders. They preside at general and annual conferences, make annual appointments to pastoral charges, ordain deacons and elders, and have general oversight of all religious work of the church.

Conferences:

1. The *quarterly conference* is composed of the official boards of each pastoral charge and is the highest authority for local administration.

2. The *district conference* is composed of all preachers, church-school superintendents, lay leaders, heads of women's and youth organizations of each church of the area, along with others especially appointed.[2]

3. The *annual conference* is an administrative body and is the basic body of the church. It receives reports and decides questions of discipline. Here the bishop ordains candidates for the ministry. Here also all constitutional amendments are voted upon. Ministerial and lay delegates to the general conference are elected here.

4. The *general conference* is composed of delegates from the annual conferences. These delegates are chosen by ballot at the last meeting previous to the meeting of the general conference. It meets once every four years. This conference has full power to make rules, regulations, and disciplines. (See *Doctrines and Discipline of The Methodist Church*, 1944.)

This great denomination now has a rather complicated organization, beginning with a Council of Bishops, six Jurisdictional Conferences (five geographical, the sixth composed of Negro Churches), and such bodies as a Board of Publication, The Methodist Publishing House, Board of Missions and Church Extension (with Divisions of Home Missions, Woman's Division of Christian Service, Joint Division of Education and Cultivation), Board of Education, Commission on Ministerial Training, two Boards of Pensions, Board of Hospitals and Homes, Board of Temperance, Board of Lay Activities, Board

---

[2] *Discipline of The Methodist Church*, 1944, Paragraph 666: A district conference shall be composed of all preachers—traveling, superannuated or retired, supernumerary, and local—the exhorters, the church-school superintendent, from each church in the district, the district stewards, the district trustees, the district lay leader and associate lay leaders, the charge lay leaders, the district secretary or president of the women's organizations, the district director of young people's work, or adult work, of children's work and such other persons as the annual conference may determine.

of Evangelism, Commission on World Service and Finance, Commission on World Peace, Interboard Commission on Missionary Education, Commission on Public Information, Commission on Chaplains, Commission on Camp Activities, Youth Fellowship, Crusade for Christ, and the Committee on Overseas Relief. All of these boards, commissions, and committees are headed by bishops, with clergymen and lay people serving in many capacities within each section and subdivision. The main executive offices are located in New York City, Chicago, and Nashville, Tennessee.

WHAT—IN BELIEF?

The doctrine of The Methodist Church is found in the *Articles of Religion,* Wesley's published sermons, and Wesley's *Notes on the New Testament.* These emphasize such beliefs as: the Trinity, the fall of man, the need of repentance, freedom of the will, sanctification, future punishments and rewards, and the sufficiency of the Scriptures for salvation.

Baptism.   Baptism is administered to both infants and adults. Sprinkling is the preferred form, but the adult may choose sprinkling, pouring, or immersion, as he pleases.

The other sacrament is the Lord's Supper, which is merely a memorial.

Church Membership.   The chief condition which is required is "a desire to flee from the wrath to come and to be saved from their sins." It is expected that each member will lead an honorable life and abstain from all things which would not be to the glory of God.

Creed.   Bishop John H. Vincent has given this summary of Methodist beliefs in the following points:

1. I believe that all men are sinners.
2. I believe that God the Father loves all men and hates all sin.
3. I believe that Jesus Christ died for all men, to make possible their salvation from sin and to make sure the salvation of all who believe in him.
4. I believe that the Holy Spirit is given to all men to enlighten and to incline them to repent of their sins and to believe in the Lord Jesus Christ.

5. I believe that all who repent of their sins and believe in the Lord Jesus Christ receive the forgiveness of sins. This is *justification*.

6. I believe that all who receive forgiveness of sins are at the same time made new creatures in Christ Jesus. This is *regeneration*.

7. I believe that all who are made new creatures in Christ Jesus are accepted as children of God. This is *adoption*.

8. I believe that all who are accepted as the children of God may receive the inward assurance of the Holy Spirit to that fact. This is the *witness of the Spirit*.

9. I believe that all who truly desire and seek it may love God with all their heart, soul, mind, strength and their neighbors as themselves. This is *entire sanctification*.

10. I believe that all who persevere to the end, and only these, shall be saved in heaven forever.[3]

HELPS FOR STUDY

Written Work

1. Give the history of The Methodist Church.
2. What did John Wesley do for this Church?
3. Define the following terms according to Methodist ruling: church membership, church officers, conferences.
4. What do the following terms mean: justification, regeneration, adoption, witness of the Spirit, entire sanctification?

Oral Discussion

1. Is The Methodist Church the largest Protestant denomination?
2. Do Christians today lack zeal?
3. Is it wrong to appeal to one's emotions?
4. Why has The Methodist Church been the champion of the common people in the social and economic areas of life?
5. How has this denomination "solved" the race issue?

Special Assignments

1. Study the life of John Wesley.
2. Outline Chapter VI of Brown's *The Larger Faith*.
3. Read the Methodist hymn, "Jesus, Lover of My Soul."
4. Find out something about the following men: Samuel Wesley, Thomas Maxfield, George Whitefield, Jabez Bunting.

---

[3] For additional information see *The Methodist Primer*, by Charles Claude Seleman; *Methodists United for Action*, by John R. Mott; and *The Methodist Church in Belief and Action*, by John M. Moore.

28

THE CHURCH OF HARMONY
. . . the Universalist Church[1]

That nothing walks with aimless feet,
That not one life shall be destroyed,
Or cast as rubbish to the void
When God has made His pile complete.
ALFRED TENNYSON

WHEN AND WHERE?

The Universalist denomination is of modern origin. It is confined mostly to America and embraces only a portion of those who hold Universalist views.

This denomination began with the arrival of John Murray, of London, in Good Luck, New Jersey, in September, 1770. He preached in New York, Pennsylvania, and Massachusetts and as a result societies sprang up in these states which held to the Universalist view. A church was built by Murray at Gloucester, Massachusetts, in 1780. The name selected for this church was "The Independent Christian Society, commonly called 'Universalists.' "

The first convention of this body was held at Oxford, Massachusetts, in 1785, but not a great deal was accomplished outside of making a move towards a definite organization. The second convention was held in Philadelphia, in 1790. Here was drawn up and published the first Universalist profession of faith, an outline plan of church organization was made, and the

---

[1] Approximate membership in the United States, 50,000.

convention approved the congregational form of polity. The third convention was held at Oxford, in 1793, and this developed, as years passed, into the Convention of the New England States and finally into the present organization, the general convention. In 1870 a plan of organization and a manual of administration were adopted which the denomination still uses.

WHY?

We all believe that "God is love." The Universalists, however, could not make this belief coincide with the Calvinistic God and so they have rejected the latter emphasis altogether. They preach a message of forgiving love as the central quality of divinity. They will not have evil defeat a loving God who is Father of all mankind. And as Henry Kalloch Rowe says:

Enough of them had thus reacted against the hopeless doctrines of predestination and future punishment to organize Universalist churches.

In other words, these people refuse to send anyone to hell, for they believe that the Father of Love has created no such place for his children. The Universalist Church is, therefore, an instrument to perpetuate this central belief.

WHAT—IN ORGANIZATION?

The Universalist Church has adopted the congregational form of organization. Each local parish or society is free in the management of its own temporal affairs, in conducting its worship, and in the choice of officers, including the pastor. The different parishes are organized into state conventions and delegates from the state convention compose the general convention.

In the *Organization and Administration Manual for Universalist Churches* the following statement is made regarding the general organization:

Historically, our church is a pure democracy; but its polity is congregational. First come the parishes or churches which voluntarily unite in state or national conventions and delegate to these whatever powers they possess.

By such process our church organization has come to be constituted, on the same plan as the United States of America, as follows:

1. The general convention, having jurisdiction over all Universalist clergymen and denominational organization.

2. State conventions, exercising within state or provincial limits a similar jurisdiction, subject to the general convention.

3. Individual churches, composed of persons organized for religious improvement and the support of public worship.

Church Membership. The admission to membership is not the same in all churches. But, on the whole, the uniform custom is to require the Winchester Profession or the Statement of Essential Principles as basic historic symbols. Most of the churches have a covenant, but much freedom is given the individual as to his interpretation of it.

Sacraments. This denomination observes the Lord's Supper four times a year. Baptism is either by immersion or sprinkling, and is administered both to infants and adults. Both of these sacraments are used only as symbols. Only ordained ministers are permitted to administer these sacraments.[2]

WHAT—IN BELIEF?

The Universalist Church has no creed, but at the general convention held at Winchester, New Hampshire, in September, 1803, a profession of faith was formulated. This was accepted by the convention, but without ecclesiastical authority. However, today it is acknowledged by the denomination at large as an expression of its faith. It is as follows:

We believe that the Holy Scriptures of the Old and New Testaments contain a revelation of the character of God and of duty, interest, and final destination of mankind.

We believe that there is one God, whose nature is Love, revealed

---

[2] See *The Beginnings of the Universalist Church*, by A. Gertrude Earle; also *Charter and By-Laws of the Universalist Church* (Universalist Publishing House, Boston, Massachusetts).

in one Lord Jesus Christ, by one Holy Spirit of Grace, who will finally restore the whole family of mankind to holiness and happiness.

We believe that holiness and true happiness are inseparably connected, and that believers ought to be careful to maintain order and practise good works; for these things are good and profitable unto men.

The "Statement of Essential Principles" was adopted by the general convention held in Boston, October, 1899, and was made the condition of fellowship. The principles are as follows:

1. The Universal Fatherhood of God.
2. The spiritual authority and leadership of his Son, Jesus Christ.
3. The trustworthiness of the Bible as containing a revelation from God.
4. The certainty of just retribution for sin.
5. The final harmony of all souls with God.

HELPS FOR STUDY

Written Work

1. Give the history of the Universalist Church.
2. Why did the Universalist Church organize?
3. What kind of an organization has it?
4. What are their five essentials of belief?

Oral Discussion

1. What did Jesus say about the future life?
2. Where is hell?
3. Do sinners have a chance after death to repent and believe?
4. Where did sin come from?
5. Why has the Universalist Church remained weak?

Special Assignments

1. Find the number of times Jesus referred to the future punishment of the wicked.

2. Look up the biography of John Murray.
3. Sing the Universalist hymn, "The Sweet By and By."
4. Read Emerson's "Essay on Compensation."
5. Show that there is a universal hope of a salvation after death.

29

THE CHURCH OF REASON
. . . the Unitarian Church[1]

> He drew a circle to shut me out,
> Heretic, rebel, a thing to flout,
> But Love and I had the wit to win,
> We drew a circle that took him in.
>
> EDWIN MARKHAM

WHEN AND WHERE?

The Unitarianism of today originated in the first half century of the Protestant Reformation. During the sixteenth century many independent thinkers of Italy and Switzerland, along with a few Anabaptist leaders, held to the Unitarian belief. They were also known under the names of Arianism and Socinianism.

In England there were such men as Newton, Locke, and Milton who held Unitarian views, but no movement toward forming a distinct denomination was made until late in the eighteenth century.

In America, Unitarianism resulted from a division in the Congregational Church. This Church had left its members free to believe as they pleased; requiring no set doctrine, but only a short and simple covenant. As doctrinal changes arose, many of the churches in eastern Massachusetts slowly moved toward the Unitarian beliefs. In the second half of the eighteenth century, many of the most important and oldest churches accepted

---

[1] Approximate membership in the United States, 75,000.

these beliefs. However, the first church completely to accept the new doctrines was the Episcopal King's Chapel at Boston, in 1785. At first these churches were called "Liberal Christians," but later (1815) the name "Unitarian" became attached to them.

The real cleavage between the Congregational and the Unitarian bodies took place when Henry Ware, a true liberal, was elected professor of theology at Harvard University, in 1805. More and more the liberals were refused fellowship in the Congregational churches. When William Ellery Channing of Boston preached a sermon at Baltimore, in 1819, which defended and defined the Unitarian point of view, it was accepted as their platform.

In 1825, a missionary and promotion organization was formed which was called the American Unitarian Association. This made the Unitarians a separate denomination. In 1865, a national conference was organized and the period of aggressive denominational life was begun.

WHY?

To answer this question it will be very fitting to give Channing's definition of the true Church. He says:

By his Church our Saviour does not mean a party bearing the name of a human leader, distinguished by a form or an opinion, and on the ground of this distinction, denying the name and character of Christians to all but themselves. . . . These are the true church—men made better, made holy, virtuous by his religion—men who, hoping in his promises, keep his commands.

J. B. Bury, in his *History of Freedom of Thought*, gives us the answer to this question when he says:

We owe the modern principle of toleration to the Italian group of Reformers, who rejected the doctrine of the Trinity, and were the fathers of Unitarianism.

Unitarians are, therefore, those who hold to the Arian views of Jesus, believing in the oneness of God, and accept no creed or doctrine (not even the Scriptures) as the foundation of their faith. Truth alone is their foundation. During the process of time an organization has been built upon this foundation and it has come to be known as the Unitarian Church.

WHAT—IN ORGANIZATION?

The Unitarians have a congregational form of organization. Each church is separate and independent. For the purpose of fellowship and mutual counsel they meet in local, state, and general conferences. The International Congress attempts

. . . to open communication with those in all lands who are striving to unite pure religion and perfect liberty, and to increase fellowship and cooperation among them.

The other organizations of this denomination are the American Unitarian Association (a missionary society), the Alliance of Unitarian Women, the Unitarian Sunday School Society, the Young People's Religious Union, the Laymen's League, and the Unitarian Temperance Society.[2]

WHAT—IN BELIEF?

Unitarians have no creed. The constitution of the general conference states that:

These churches accept the religion of Jesus, holding in accordance with his teaching that practical religion is summed up in the love to God and love to man.

The general consensus of their belief can be put in the following points:

1. The unipersonality of God.
2. The strict humanity of Jesus.
3. The perfectibility of human character.
4. The natural character of the Bible.
5. The ultimate salvation of all souls.

Nothing is better, in order to understand the beliefs of this denomination, than *Leaflet 15*, published by the British and

---

[2] See the leaflet, *Introducing Unitarianism,* by John Nicholls Booth (The Beacon Press, Boston, Massachusetts).

Foreign Unitarian Association. Here are a few of the most important questions and answers:

1. *What do Unitarians themselves regard as the central idea, the kernel of their faith?*

Belief in the divine nature of man, as opposed to the doctrine of total depravity.

2. *Why do Unitarians reject the doctrine of the Trinity?*

Because it is unintelligible and contrary to reason. It is nowhere taught in the New Testament. The only text in the Authorized Version which seemed to teach the doctrine (I John 5: 7) was omitted as spurious in the Revised Version by the unanimous concurrence of the revision committee, who were nearly all Trinitarian scholars.

3. *How can Unitarians be Christians while denying the divinity of Jesus?*

They deny the deity of Jesus, but not his divinity. Indeed, they specially emphasize his divinity as a real and personal quality inherent in his humanity.

4. *What ground is there for believing in the divine nature of man as sharing in the nature of God and of Jesus Christ?*

It is a doctrine that agrees with the Master's own teaching as found in the New Testament, and is both simple and rational.

5. *What do Unitarians believe about God?*

That God is the Father of every human soul; that his nature includes wisdom, power, and goodness, and that he is infinitely forgiving.

From this there naturally follows the belief that all men are brothers.

6. *When Unitarians teach "salvation by character rather than by belief," what do they mean?*

That character is an end, not a means. That salvation is being saved from sin here, not from punishment hereafter. Unitarians believe that it was the mission of Jesus to save us from sin itself by helping us to become good men and women; that the evil we have to fear is sin, not punishment for sin; and that the greatest blessing attainable is goodness itself, not any reward for goodness.

7. *It is said that the Unitarians do not believe in the Bible. Is this true?*

They do not believe in the infallibility of the Bible taught in the doctrine of "plenary inspiration." This doctrine has hidden much of the real power and beauty of the Bible, since it places every passage on a dead level; putting, for instance, the gloomy pessimism of Ecclesiastes ("all is vanity") on a plane with the manly optimism of Paul ("as having nothing yet possessing all things"). The Bible is really not a book, but a library, written by many authors at different times. But Unitarians believe much of the Bible to be inspired in the truest sense, because, full of the utterances of inspired souls, that is, of men who lived in conscious communion with God.

Unitarians do not think it at all reasonable to regard some portions of the Old Testament (such as the story of the murder of Sisera) as having the same value, and deserving the same reverence, as the words of Jesus in the Sermon on the Mount.

8. *Why do Unitarians disbelieve in hell and in everlasting punishment?*

Because, among other reasons, to believe in hell, as usually understood by orthodoxy, is to deny the wisdom and power and, above all, the goodness of God. This doctrine teaches that evil is stronger than good, and will conquer God, since it maintains that many beings will live forever in sin and suffering, God himself having been unable to save them. Even if some of the various writings of the New Testament supported it, faith in God and goodness would forbid our believing it.

9. *Do Unitarians believe that all men, the good and the bad alike, will after death be received into a region of blessedness?*

By no means. They believe that Heaven is a state rather than a place; and that Heaven and hell (the real hell) may often begin in this life. They believe that Heaven is inseparable from a life of goodness and hell from a life of sin; and that the mere change from one stage of existence to another does not in itself effect a sudden transformation in the character. They believe that growth and development will go on forever, and that all suffering, whether here or hereafter, is reformatory and educational, and not vindictive. In time the wisdom and love of God will triumph over all the wilfulness and weakness of man, and will eventually lead all souls to goodness and to communion with himself.

10. *What reason have the Unitarians to believe that all souls will finally be saved?*

Because to doubt it would be to doubt that perfect goodness of God which is taught by Jesus. If we believe with him that God is our Father; that we are His children, and that God loves every soul

He has created, then we must believe that He has created us for goodness, and that we shall become in time all that He intends us to be.

Clayton R. Bowen, in *Why Are Unitarians Disciples of Christ?* makes Christ seem real when he says,

Jesus is our Leader, because he walked in the same path we must tread; our Master, because we cannot choose but to follow him; our Example, because we have similar divine possibilities; our Brother, because we have the same Father. . . . We take his hand because he is one of us.

> Call him not heretic whose works attest
> His faith in goodness, by no creed confessed.
> JOHN GREENLEAF WHITTIER

HELPS FOR STUDY

Written Work

1. Give the history of the Unitarian Church.
2. Why did the Unitarians form a separate body?
3. Make an outline of their organizations.
4. What is the general consensus of their belief?

Oral Discussion

1. Was Jesus merely a man?
2. Can one become too critical for his own good?
3. Does reasoning about religion spoil its value?
4. What relation has poetry to religion?
5. What trouble have the Unitarians had with the principles of freedom for the religious press?

Special Assignments

1. Study the life of Ralph Waldo Emerson.
2. Read some of the poetry of Lowell, Longfellow, and Bryant.
3. Outline Chapter IX of Brown's *The Larger Faith.*
4. Make a list of the Unitarian hymns.
5. Show the influence of Locke and Priestly on Unitarianism.
6. Read something about James Martineau (1805 to 1900).
7. What influence has Unitarianism had on Christian thought?

30

THE CHURCH OF UNITY
. . . the Disciples[1]

Henceforth, please God, forever I forego
The yoke of men's opinions. I will be
Light-hearted as a bird, and live with God.
I find Him in the bottom of my heart,
I hear continually His voice therein.

RALPH WALDO EMERSON

WHEN AND WHERE?

During the revival movements in the early part of the nineteenth century there arose a few people who stood for the Bible alone, without the aid of creeds or formulas. Thomas Campbell, a member of the Secession branch of the Presbyterian Church in Ireland, was one of the leaders of these people. He came to the United States in 1807 and settled in western Pennsylvania. Finding many people in this section without any direct church affiliations he invited them to join in his services. As a result, he and his son, Alexander Campbell, formed an organization called the "Christian Association of Washington, Pennsylvania." However, it was not the wish of these leaders that this association might become a distinct denomination, for denominations to them were "a horrid evil, fraught with many evils."

Because of their disbelief in infant baptism the Baptists had a great liking for this Christian fellowship. Upon the invitation

---

[1] Approximate membership, 1,900,000.

of the Redstone Baptist Association, Alexander Campbell and
his followers entered this association in 1813, thus becoming a
part of the Baptist denomination. But Mr. Campbell did not
get along very well with his Baptist friends. His paper, the
Christian Baptist (1823), caused widespread opposition against
him, and henceforth Baptist churches began to disaffiliate
his followers. Mr. Davis, the historian for the Disciples, says:

No exact day can be named as the time of this sad occurrence
[the separation], for it came about gradually and consumed several years in its consummation; but we may date it 1830. After this
the followers of Mr. Campbell were called Christians, or Disciples
of Christ, or the Christian Church, the legal title being the Church
of Christ at such and such a place.

At the present time a joint committee of Baptists and Disciples
is exploring the possibilities of a reunion. Already several
projects of a mutual nature are being carried out.

The growth of this body has been very rapid especially in
Ohio, Tennessee, and Missouri. The period directly after the
Civil War was one of great expansion. It now ranks high in
the list of Protestant denominations.

WHY?

This denomination believes in restoration rather than reformation. It was the desire of this body, in the first place, to
restore primitive Christianity, with all its beliefs and practices.
It maintained that:

. . . nothing ought to be received into the faith or worship of the
Church nor be made a test of communion among Christians that
is not as old as the New Testament.

Therefore, since the Disciples could not agree with the sectarian spirit of the Church or with the creeds and beliefs it had
made, they purposed to return to the pattern of the first church,
as found in the New Testament.

WHAT—IN ORGANIZATION?

The Disciples' churches are congregational in organization.

Each church elects its own officers and has entire control over its own organization. There is no outside ecclesiastical authority.

Candidates for membership are received upon profession of faith in Christ, before the pastor and congregation. Baptism by immersion follows.

The church officers are pastor, elders, and deacons. The duty of the elders is to care for the spiritual interests, while the deacons care for the financial affairs and the benevolences of the church.

Ministers are ordained by the local church. The service is conducted either by the pastor or the elders, and sometimes by a committee from neighboring churches. The minister is a member of the church in which he is pastor or evangelist. Ministerial associations are formed for mutual help and general supervision, but they have no authority.

To carry out their world-wide program the Disciples have an "International Convention of Disciples of Christ." This convention is composed of individual members whose standing is personal rather than representative. It has no authority over the local churches, and they may accept or reject, as they see fit, the recommendations made by it.

For mutual help, the churches meet in district and state conventions; and these, like all the rest, have no ecclesiastical authority.

In accordance with the principles that have been emphasized in their history, the Disciples of Christ, individually, in their local church organization, in their organized societies, and in their denominational relations, have constantly sought to secure the overcoming of denominational distinctions and the unity of the church in its broadest sense. They are thus represented in the various inter-denominational movements.—*U. S. Census Report.*

WHAT—IN BELIEF?

In general, the beliefs of the Disciples can be summed up in the following points:

1. They accept the Old and New Testaments as divinely inspired.

2. They accept the Bible as their rule of faith and life.

3. They hold to the belief in the Trinity while urging a simple usage of New Testament phraseology as to the godhead.

4. They believe Christ to be really the Son of God.

5. They are convinced that the Holy Spirit is at work in the world today.

6. They believe that sin has alienated every soul from its Maker.

7. They feel that baptism and the Lord's Supper are divine ordinances.

8. They feel it to be a sacred duty to keep the Lord's day.

9. They believe that holiness is a necessity for every believer.

10. They believe in the final judgment, with its reward to the righteous and punishment to the wicked.

Their distinctive beliefs are as follows:

1. Feeling that "to believe and to do none other things than those enjoined by our Lord and His Apostles must be infallibly safe," they aim, "to restore in faith and spirit and practice the Christianity of Christ and His Apostles as found on the pages of the New Testament."

2. Affirming that "the sacred Scriptures as given by God answer all purposes of a rule of faith and practice, and a law for the government of the church, and that human creeds and confessions of faith spring out of controversy and, instead of being bonds of unity, tend to division and strife," they reject all such creeds and confessions.

3. They place especial emphasis upon "the Divine Sonship of Jesus, as the fundamental fact of Holy Scripture, the essential creed of Christianity, and the one article of faith in order to receive baptism and church membership."

4. Believing that in the Scriptures "a clear distinction is made between the law and the gospel," they "do not regard the Old and New Testaments as of equally binding authority upon Christians," but that "the New Testament is as perfect a constitution for the

worship, government, and discipline of the New Testament Church as the Old was for the Old Testament Church."

5. While claiming for themselves the New Testament names of "Christians," or "Disciples," "they do not deny that others are Christians or that other churches are Churches of Christ."

6. Accepting the divine personality of the Holy Spirit through whose agency regeneration is begun, they hold that men "must hear, believe, repent, and obey the gospel to be saved."

7. Repudiating any doctrine of "baptismal regeneration" and insisting that there is no other prerequisite to regeneration than confession of faith with the whole heart in the personal living Christ, they regard baptism by immersion "as one of the items of the original systems," and as "commanded in order to the remission of sins."

8. Following this apostolic model, the Disciples celebrate the Lord's Supper on each Lord's day, "not as a sacrament, but as a memorial feast," from which no sincere follower of Christ of whatever creed or church connection is excluded.

9. The Lord's day with the Disciples is not the Sabbath, but a New Testament institution, consecrated by apostolic example.

10. The Church of Christ is a divine institution; sects are unscriptural and unapostolic, and the sect name, spirit, and life should give place to the union and cooperation that distinguished the church of the New Testament.[2]

> Great day of God, all glorious;
> Great day of Peace, so blest;
> The thought of Thee brings gladness,
> And dilates every breast.
> Great day of one religion,
> When all are understood;
> One faith in Life Eternal,
> One God, one Brotherhood.

LOUISE R. WAITE

[2] See for reference: *The Disciples of Christ*, by Alonzo W. Fortune; *You and Christian Baptism* and *You and the Lord's Supper*, both by Harold F. Humbert; *That for Which We Stand*, by P. S. Snodgrass (General Headquarters, Disciples of Christ, 516 K. of P. Building, Indianapolis, Indiana).

HELPS FOR STUDY

Written Work

1. Give the history of the Disciples.
2. What did this body propose to do?
3. What is the organization of the denomination?
4. Give the beliefs of the Disciples.

Oral Discussion

1. Believing as they do in Christian unity, why have the Disciples not been able to unite with other Christian bodies?
2. Why do Christians have to be baptized if baptism is not a saving ordinance?
3. What has the Church done for America?
4. Is it an easy thing to be a disciple of Christ today?
5. How can Christianity be made popular?

Special Assignments

1. Study the life of Thomas Campbell.
2. Attend a Disciples church.
3. Write a paper on the value of denominations.
4. Show the relation of this body to the Baptists.
5. Discover the contribution of this denomination to Christianity.

31

OTHER RELIGIOUS GROUPS

Our little systems have their day,
They have their day and cease to be;
They are but broken lights of thee,
And thou, O Lord, art more than they.

TENNYSON

THE ADVENTISTS

The Adventists are a body of people who believe in the personal return of Christ to this earth some time in the near future. William Miller, at one time a Baptist, founded the movement in Massachusetts, in 1831. As the result of Miller's unfulfilled prophecies, concerning the second coming of Christ, the body became divided into six divisions, each still holding the same views as formerly but setting no exact date for the return of Christ.[1]

The most important division of this body is the Seventh-day Adventists. This branch was organized in New Hampshire, in 1845, by some of Miller's followers. It is now organized into conferences with annual meetings. Stressing diet and health, it has built a number of sanitariums, one of the most outstanding being at Battle Creek. Membership is drawn from most of the states, and missionary work is conducted in Europe, Asia, Africa, and Australia.

---

[1] The Church of God is an important Adventist group. It represents churches molding premillennial views organized (1921) into a general conference with headquarters in Oregon, Illinois.

CHURCH OF THE BRETHREN

The Church of the Brethren grew out of the Pietistic Movement, being founded in Schwarzenau, Germany, in 1708. As a result of persecution, because of its opposition to the formal religion of the state churches, a congregation came to Germantown, Pennsylvania, in 1719 and established a church. From there the movement spread to the west and the south.

It is an extremely democratic church, with all members having an equal vote. Delegates are sent to annual district conferences and the General Conference. The church has no creed, but accepts the New Testament as its rule of faith and practice. It holds that only willing believers are to be baptized by immersion, that no member should take part in war, that all should live a simple life and be temperate, that class distinctions are wrong, and that right living is superior to creeds. It has distinguished itself by its extensive world relief program, particularly in its origin of the Heifers for Relief project.[2]

THE CHRISTIAN SCIENTISTS

This denomination was founded in 1876 by Mary Baker Eddy. Its first church—the First Church of Christ, Scientist, in Boston—was organized in 1879. This became the "Mother Church" of many branch churches which were founded, both in America and Europe, especially in the large cities.

The services of this church consist of readings from the *Bible* and from Mrs. Eddy's *Science and Health*, hymns, prayers, and the benediction. At the midweek service testimonies and experiences are given. There are no pastors, but instead two Readers, namely: the First Reader (of *Science and Health*) and the Second Reader (of the *Bible*). The "Galilean Breakfast" takes the place of the Lord's Supper.

Mrs. Eddy's book, *Science and Health*, is the basis for the belief of this body. It is the "key" to the Scriptures. It reveals unto man the science of God, the only Reality.

---

[2] See *Minutes of the Annual Conference of the Church of the Brethren* (Headquarters, Church of the Brethren, 22 South State Street, Elgin Illinois).

One of the most remarkable achievements of this body is the publication of *The Christian Science Monitor*, recognized as one of the top daily newspapers of the nation.

EVANGELICAL UNITED BRETHREN CHURCH

This is the baby among the denominations. It had its birth at Johnstown, Pennsylvania, in November 16, 1946, when the consummation of organic union between the Evangelical Church and the Church of the United Brethren in Christ took place. Jacob Albright was the founder of the former, and Philip William Otterbein of the latter. Both churches had their beginnings in Pennsylvania, in the evangelistic movement of the early nineteenth century. The government of this new denomination is Methodistic and its doctrine Arminian.

This Evangelical United Brethren Church has a constituent membership in the United States and Canada of approximately 700,000, with an additional 125,000 in the mission field abroad. There are some 4,700 churches and 3,500 ministers. Under the basis of union no changes have been made in doctrine.

EVANGELICAL AND REFORMED CHURCH

On June 26, 1934, in Cleveland, Ohio, through a union of the Evangelical Synod of North America and the Reformed Church in the United States, this denomination came into existence. The most interesting part about this union was the fact that it united first, and left all the details of union to a later date. The constitution was finally declared in effect at the General Synod meeting at Lancaster, Pennsylvania, in June, 1940. The boards of the two bodies were merged on February 1, 1941.

The new organization consists of the General Synod (triennial), the executive officers, General Council, Department of United Promotion, Board of United Promotion, Board of National Missions, Board of International Missions, Board of Christian Education and Publication, Board of Business Management, Board of Pensions and Relief, and several commissions.

This denomination has a European background, mostly German. It has its headquarters in three areas: Philadelphia, Chicago, and St. Louis. There are approximately 700,000 members, with 2,806 churches, about a thousand of these being in Pennsylvania. Its form of government is similar to the Presbyterian Church. Authority is vested in the synod, rather than in the local church.[3]

THE CHURCH OF THE NEW JERUSALEM (SWEDENBORGIAN)

This Church was founded by Robert Hindmarsh, of London, in 1782, when he, with a few associates, met to study the teachings of Emanuel Swedenborg. As the association grew in size, it was named the Church of the New Jerusalem, after the New Jerusalem of the Apocalypse. The first Swedenborgian society in America was organized at Baltimore, in 1792. Its government is both congregational and episcopal, as each local society is self-governing; but general pastors (corresponding to bishops in Episcopal churches) have oversight of certain districts. The service is liturgical, and the *Book of Worship* prepared by the general convention is used.

According to Swedenborg, who claimed to live in the spiritual world, the Church came to an end in 1757, and the new dispensation would begin when the Church of the New Jerusalem (prophesied in the Revelation) would finally be realized. All the doctrines of this church are based upon the writings of Swedenborg and deal mostly with the spiritual world.

PENTECOSTAL BODIES

Many relatively small organizations hold Pentecostal views, particularly those of sanctification and holiness. Most important of these groups are the Pentecostal Fire-baptized Holiness Church, the United Pentecostal Church, Incorporated, the In-

---

[3] See *My Church—Whence, What, Whither* (Evangelical and Reformed Church, 1505 Race Street, Philadelphia 2, Pennsylvania). *Know Your Church*, by Paul T. Stonesifer. *What Our Church Believes. The Basis of Union of the Congregational Christian Churches and the Evangelical and Reformed Church* (Issued by a joint committee of the two Churches).

ternational Pentecostal Assemblies, the Pentecostal Assemblies of the World, the Pentecostal Church of God in America, the United Pentecostal Church, Incorporated, the Calvary Pentecostal Church, Incorporated, the Pentecostal Holiness Church, and the Pilgrim Holiness Church.[4]

Jehovah's Witnesses

While not organized into a formal denomination, Jehovah's Witnesses are well known throughout the world for their refusal to salute the flag, to participate in war, and their insistence that all of their members have the official standing of ministers. In all of these matters they have taken their case to the Supreme Court of the United States.

Although not a sect or denomination, Jehovah's Witnesses are associated with the Watch Tower Bible and Tract Society, and with the International Bible Students Association. Pastor Charles T. Russell was their first leader. Upon his death, in 1916, Judge Joseph F. Rutherford became president of the organization. After Judge Rutherford's death, in 1942, he was succeeded in office by Nathan H. Knorr.[5]

The Mormons, or the Latter-day Saints

Joseph Smith founded this body April 6, 1830, at Fayette, Seneca County, New York. His reason for doing it was that the Lord had told him that all the churches were wrong and that the true gospel would soon be revealed unto men. Three years after this experience an "angel" came to him, while he was in prayer in his room, and revealed to him (September 22, 1827) the hiding place of some gold plates on which was written the true word of God. With the aid of certain supernatural "stones in silver bows" his vision was clear to translate what was written on the plates. When the work was finished the plates were re-

[4] See *General Constitution and By-Laws, The Pentecostal Church of God of America* (General Headquarters, 1100 Prospect Avenue, Kansas City 1, Missouri).

[5] See *1948 Yearbook of Jehovah's Witnesses* (Watch Tower Bible and Tract Society, Brooklyn, New York).

turned to the angel and the *Book of Mormon* was published.
It has fifteen divisions, each claimed to have been written by
a different hand, which gives the history of certain imaginary
races which once lived in prehistoric America.

After Smith's death the organization divided, but the largest
part followed the leadership of Brigham Young. Under his
guidance the organization was transferred to Great Salt Lake,
Utah, where it has since remained.

The Mormon beliefs are in general:

1. That the *Bible* "in so far as it is correctly translated"
should be accepted.
2. That the *Book of Mormon* is the word of God.
3. That there is a present and progressive revelation.
4. That polygamy may be practiced.
5. That God is man (Adam) exalted.
6. That those who build large polygamous establishments
will be made as gods in the after life.
7. That the "gods" multiply their progeny through their
"celestial wives."
8. That baptism by immersion is necessary to salvation.
9. That the Lord's Supper should be observed every Sunday.
10. That obedience to the priesthood is of the first importance.

THE MENNONITES

This body is the successor of the Anabaptist movement.
Menno Simons, a converted Roman Catholic priest, was their
leader; and he successfully organized the scattered congregations of the Anabaptists in the Netherlands and Germany. In
America the Mennonites first settled in Pennsylvania (1683)
and ever since this state has been their greatest stronghold.

The Mennonite Confession of Faith, adopted in 1632, contains such doctrines as the Trinity, the fall of man, the atone-
ment, non-resistance, the forbidding of the use of oaths, baptism to believers by pouring, the Lord's Supper observed twice
a year, foot washing, and the "kiss of peace." In the last two

ceremonies the sexes are separated. Holding office and the bearing of arms for the State is also discouraged.

Bishops or elders exercise administrative oversight in districts and the pastors are chosen from the congregation which they are to serve, usually by lot. Deacons are chosen in the same manner.

Delegates to the quadrennial session of the General Conference of the Mennonite Brethren in Christ Church voted at Potsdam, Ohio, November 17, 1947, to change the name of their denomination to that of the United Missionary Church.

THE MORAVIANS

This organization traces its history back to John Huss, the Moravian reformer, who was burned as a "heretic" at the Council of Constance, in 1415. Count Zinzendorf of Saxony became their protector and leader in 1722, and under his influence the "Brethren's Church" became reorganized, after the Thirty Years' War. Ten years later this Moravian Church launched a world-wide program of foreign missions.

The Moravian Church was first planted in America by immigrants in 1735, in Georgia. Later settlements were made in Pennsylvania, North Carolina, and Ohio. Here they did active missionary work among the Indians.

The Moravian Church subscribes to the Apostles' Creed and uses a variety of liturgies. It practices infant baptism. It has a membership of about 40,000 in America and 260,000 throughout the world.

The organization is divided into Provinces, each administered by a synod. In doctrine, Moravians emphasize the love of God, the second coming of Christ, his divinity, resurrection, prayer, and the inner testimony of the spirit. Moravians are noted for their beautiful outdoor Easter services.

THE NAZARENES

This body is the result of the fusion of several Holiness Associations in the eastern part of the country, the Church of the Nazarenes (in California), and the Holiness Church of

Christ, which took place in 1907. This Church has been closely connected with the Methodist movement, both in type of organization and in belief. It has its general assembly, general superintendents, elders, and evangelists. In doctrine, it lays emphasis on the depravity of the human race, on entire sanctification, and on the second coming of Christ. It opposes the use of alcoholic drinks and tobacco, and membership in secret societies. It leads all other denominations in per capita giving.

THE SALVATION ARMY

William Booth (at one time a Methodist minister) and his wife, Catherine Mumford Booth, were engaged in mission work in the East End of London. One day, in describing their work Mr. Booth said, "The Christian Mission is a salvation army of converted working people," and in 1878, as a result of this statement, the work came to be known under the name of the "Salvation Army."

True to its name, the organization is formed on a military basis. The officers consist of a commander in chief, a chief of staff, a lieutenant general, a captain, a lieutenant, a color sergeant, a paymaster sergeant, and other minor officers. All officers wear uniforms, and their meeting places are called barracks. It has no ecclesiastical organization and its converts usually join evangelical churches.

The doctrines of this body are outlined in a book of doctrine and discipline prepared by William Booth. It is very largely Methodistic in its belief and practice. The Salvation Army was extended to America in 1880. It is now represented in sixty countries. It has come to be recognized as one of the greatest humanitarian organizations in all the world.

THE SPIRITUALISTS

The "Fox sisters," who lived at Hydersville, near Rochester, New York, are given the credit for starting this movement in America. In 1848 their séances caused a great deal of excitement, and, as a result, many circles were formed which sent for mediums to inform the people of the latest discovery.

This society claims to be able to communicate with departed spirits who are living in the spiritual world. The answers received from these spirits are expressed in raps, sounds, moving of furniture, and different signs, which are interpreted by the medium. The Spiritualists have organized into societies and the National Spiritualist's Association at Washington, D. C. (1893). They have ordained and lay ministers, and mediums. At their public meetings, baptisms, and funerals, they have a prepared ritual.

JEWISH CONGREGATIONS

Jews arrived in the colonies some time before 1650. The first congregation is recorded in 1656, the Shearth Israel of New York City. The congregational and rabbinical organizations at the present time are the Union of American Hebrew Congregations, the Union of Orthodox Jewish Congregations, the United Synagogue of America, the Central Conference of American Rabbis, the Rabbinical Assembly of America, the Rabbinical Council of America, the Union of Orthodox Rabbis of the United States and Canada, and the Synagogue Council of America.

> But God is never so far off
>   As even to be near;
> He is within: our spirit is
>   The home He holds most dear.
> To think of Him as by our side
>   Is almost as untrue,
> As to remove His throne beyond
>   Those skies of starry blue.
>
> FREDERICK W. FABER

HELPS FOR STUDY

Written Work

1. What special beliefs do the Adventists hold?
2. What is Christian Science based on?
3. For what is the Church of the Brethren known?

4. Why do we have an Evangelical and Reformed denomination?
5. What does the Swedenborgian Church stress?
6. In what way are the Pentecostal bodies all alike?
7. What do you think of Jehovah's Witnesses?
8. Give the beliefs of the Mormons.
9. Who are the Mennonites?
10. For what are the Moravians noted?
11. What do the Nazarenes believe?
12. Give the history of the Salvation Army.
13. What do the Spiritualists believe?
14. How are the Jews organized?

Oral Discussion

1. Should Sundays be made different from the other days of the week?
2. What effect does the mind have on the body?
3. Who is God? Where is God?
4. Is the *Bible* the only book of God?
5. Why do not all of these many different denominations work through the Federal Council of the Church of Christ in America?
6. Is missionary work worth while?
7. What good does the Salvation Army do?
8. Why are denominations able to unite on foreign-mission fields when they are not able to unite here at home?

Special Assignments

1. Draw a chart showing the development of denominations.
2. Make a comparison of the denominations.
3. Write a thousand-word essay on the value of the study of the evolution of denominations.
4. Show the value of nonecclesiastical bodies to Christianity.

32

WORKING TOGETHER
The Denominations in
Co-operative Action

The denominations are co-operating to a far greater extent than most people realize. In hundreds of communities throughout the nation they hold union services, have united relief appeals, and work through a Council of Churches. This is also true on area and state levels. Most of us are aware of the fact that young people, laymen and women, have many joint projects and programs which break over denominational lines. But the place where the largest amount of actual co-operation is being accomplished is on the national level, and it is here that it is the least understood.

CHURCH WORLD SERVICE

All too few Protestants are familiar, for example, with the constructive work being done through the various departments of the Federal Council of the Churches of Christ in America. They fail to realize that here we have a remarkable demonstration of actual denominations federated in a Christian service council. The same is true of the interdenominational world relief organization, Church World Service. This is not a separate organization, but the denominations working together through a common channel. Often we are apt to think of national church agencies—if we think of them at all—as being outside bodies remote from the denominations and sometimes superimposing their will or program upon them. Such is not the case; these organizations would be helpless without the full co-operation of the boards or commissions of the various denominations. These interdenominational agencies are the servants of the Protestant churches. If we kept this more in mind, we would get far more in service and leadership. Instead of curtailing our support of interdenominational agencies, we need, as denominational groups, to work through them to a far greater extent. This applies to the World Council of Churches as much as it does to national agencies, for Protestants and the Orthodox Churches need, above everything else, complete co-operation at the point where it will do the most good.

It must be emphasized that our denominations are not so evil as many good people, who know very little of their co-operative actions, think. Here is a list of the established agencies through which they are now working together day after day and year after year:

National Protestant Council on Higher Education
Federal Council of the Churches of Christ in America
Foreign Missions Conference of North America
Home Missions Council of North America
International Council of Religious Education
Missionary Education Movement of the United States and Canada
United Council of Church Women
United Stewardship Council
World Council of Christian Education

To this list should be added the American Bible Society, the United Church Canvass, and other such interdenominational agencies as the Y.M.C.A. and the Y.W.C.A. There is both a Protestant Film Commission and a Protestant Radio Commission. When the proposed National Council of the Churches of Christ in the United States of America is organized, which will unite the agencies listed in the preceding paragraph, these two commissions will likely be incorporated within the proper division or department. In this over-all interdenominational agency, the membership will be on the basis of "communions" or denominations. Boards of the denominations will become members of the various divisions, departments, and commissions. Thus, as it should be, the foundation of this new agency will be the denominations working together.

BREAKDOWN OF DENOMINATIONAL BOUNDARIES

Still another illustration of the breakdown of denominational boundaries is seen in the United Church of Canada. The United Church, being a "conciliar" Church as contrasted with those whose government is in the hands of Bishops, has as its highest court the General Council, which meets for ten days or more every second year. In it, as in every court of the Church— Official Board, Presbytery, Conference—laymen have equal representation. Therefore, the General Council has one minister for every eighteen on the roll, with an equal number of laymen added and with Overseas Missions representation.

Those elected to General Council are called Commissioners. They are nominated by Presbyteries and elected by the Annual Conferences preceding the General Council. The retiring Moderator, the Secretary, and the Treasurer are ex-officio members.

The General Council is the legislative body of the United Church of Canada and operates under what is called the Basis of Union, which had the approval of the highest courts of the Churches forming the Union in 1925—Presbyterian, Methodist, and Congregational.

The powers of the General Council are set forth in *The Manual,* which is revised after every meeting of the Council and is the Constitution of the United Church. The Manual says: "The General Council shall have power (a) to determine the number and boundaries of the Conferences, to have oversight of them and to review their records; (b) to legislate on matters respecting the doctrine, worship, membership, and government of the Church (under specific conditions)." It also has charge of colleges of the Church and appoints Commissions, Committees and Boards; it corresponds with other Churches, and in general enacts such measures "as may tend to promote true godliness, repress immorality, preserve the unity and well-being of the Church, and advance the Kingdom of Christ throughout the world."

The Moderator is the spiritual head of the Church and holds office for two years. His duties are to give spiritual leadership to the Church; to visit the Church; to represent the Church on public occasions; and to preside at the meetings of the General Council and its Executive. He also calls together every quarter a meeting of the chairmen and secretaries of the administrative Boards of the Church for conference, and to secure the largest measure of co-operation possible in the whole work of the Church. The General Council has its permanent office at 421 Wesley Buildings, Toronto. The secretary is the chief executive officer of the Church. He holds office until a successor is appointed.

The United Church of Canada has eleven Conferences in Canada and Newfoundland (Bermuda is included in the Maritime Conference). There are 2,710 pastoral charges with 6,670 preaching places, and overseas missions in Africa, India, China, Japan, Korea, Trinidad. In 1926 the membership was 609,729 as compared with a population of 8,788,000. In 1946 it was 767,998 as compared with a population of 12,119,000, the total number of families being 518,536. During the year 1946 the membership increased by 18,624.

Some of the important commissions which have been set up during recent years are: Commission on Church, Nation, and World Order; Commission on Negotiations between the Church of England in Canada and the United Church of Canada on Reunion, and a Commission on the Ministries of Women.[1]

The Common Christian Cause

While striving for a larger degree of church unity, and rejoicing when two or more Christian bodies are able to merge their common interests in a new organization, let us not overlook the fact that we already have in the Federal Council (and all the agencies to be included in the proposed National Coun-

---

[1] Refer to *The United Church Observer*, 299 Queen Street West, Toronto, Ontario, for current information concerning the United Church of Canada.

cil) and the World Council of Churches a demonstration of our denominations working together. One of the very best ways to achieve closer Christian co-operation is to strengthen our own denomination in its relationship to great national and world movements of Christian federation. Working together on a federated basis, each denomination will be free to contribute its share to the common Christian cause, and the dangers which many of us see in a super-church organization can be avoided.

Our denominations are apparently going to be with us for some time to come. Instead of holding them up to ridicule and abuse, let us make the most of them, dedicating them to the great Christian principles and program which we as disciples of Christ have in common. May our denominations never become ends in themselves, but rather the *means* to a much larger and better kind of federated Christian service reaching out all over the world.

REFERENCE LIST

Note. The author recommends the following books to those who desire to do further study in this field. Mrs. Browning tells us how to read books in the following lines:

> Mark, there, we get no good
> By being ungenerous, even to a book,
> And calculating profits . . . so much help
> By so much reading. It is rather when
> We gloriously forget ourselves, and plunge
> Soul-forward, headlong, into a book's profound,
> Impassioned for its beauty and salt of truth—
> 'Tis then we get the right good from a book.

PART I: THE PRIMITIVE CHURCH

Angus, S.—*The Environment of Early Christianity*
Bacon, B. W.—*The Founding of the Church*
Barton, G. A.—*Jesus of Nazareth*
Bosworth, E. I.—*The Life and Teaching of Jesus*
Burton, E. D.—*The Teaching of Jesus*
Cadbury, H. J.—*Jesus: What Manner of Man*
Case, S. J.—*The Historicity of Jesus*
Cooley, W. F.—*The Aim of Jesus Christ*
Easton, B. S.—*The Pastoral Epistles*
Foakes-Jackson—*Beginnings of Christianity*
Foakes-Jackson—*Sketches in Primitive Christianity*
Fosdick, H. E.—*The Manhood of the Master*
Glover, T. R.—*The Jesus of History*
Glover, T. R.—*Paul of Tarsus*
Glover, T. R.—*Conflict of Religions within the Roman Empire*
Goodspeed, E. J.—*The Story of the New Testament*
Goodspeed, E. J.—*How to Read the Bible*
Harnack, A.—*Expansion of Christianity*
Harnack, A.—*The Sayings of Jesus*
Hill, W.—*The Apostolic Age*
Hodges, G.—*The Early Church*
Jefferson, C.—*The Character of Paul*

Kent, C. F.—*The Life and Teachings of Jesus*
Kent, C. F.—*The Work and Teaching of the Apostles*
Latourette, K. S.—*A History of the Expansion of Christianity*
Moffatt, J.—*An Introduction to the Literature of the New Testament*
Moore, E. C.—*The New Testament in the Christian Church*
Norton, F. O.—*The Rise of Christianity*
Orr, J.—*The History and Literature of the Early Church*
Penniman, J. H.—*A Book About the English Bible*
Purinton, H. R.—*The Achievement of the Master*
Purinton, H. R.—*Literature of the New Testament*
Ramsay, W. H.—*The Church and the Roman Empire to A.D. 170*
Rauschenbush, W.—*The Social Principles of Jesus*
Scott, E. F.—*Beginnings of the Church*
Simkhovitch, V. G.—*Toward the Understanding of Jesus*
Slaten, A. W.—*What Jesus Taught*
Souter, A.—*The Text and Canon of the New Testament*
Toynbee, A. J.—*A Study of History*

PART II: THE ANCIENT CATHOLIC CHURCH

Allen, J. H.—*Christian History*
Bryce, J.—*The Holy Roman Empire*
Curtis, W. A.—*History of Creeds and Confessions of Faith*
Farrar, F. W.—*Lives of the Fathers*
Firth, J. B.—*Constantine the Great*
Flick, A. C.—*The Rise of the Mediæval Church*
Gibbon, E.—*Decline and Fall of the Roman Empire*
Gray, G. Z.—*The Children's Crusade*
Hannah, I. C.—*Christian Monasticism*
Hopkins, A.—*The Apostle's Creed*
Newman, J. H.—*The Arians of the Fourth Century*
Morris, E. E.—*The Crusades*
Munro, D. C.—*History of the Middle Ages*
Rainy, R.—*The Ancient Catholic Church*
Sabatier, Paul—*Life of St. Francis*
Schaff, P.—*History of the Christian Church*
Ten Epochs of Church History
The Fathers of the Church: Vol. I, *The Apostolic Fathers*, translated by
    Francis X. Glimm, Joseph M. F. Marique, Gerald G. Walsh
Thatcher and McNeal—*A Source Book for Mediæval History*
Trench, R. C.—*Medieval Church History*
Walker, W.—*Outline of Church History*

PART III: THE PROTESTANT REFORMATION

Allen, A. G.—*Christian Institutions*
Bettenson, H.—*Documents of the Christian Church*

Froude, J. A.—*Council of Trent*
Gardiner, S. R.—*The Thirty Years' War*
Jackson, S. M.—*Works of Zwingli*
Lindsay, T. M.—*A History of the Reformation*
Luther, Martin—*Three Treatises*
McGiffert, A. C.—*Martin Luther*
Newman, A. H.—*A Manual of Church History*
Nichols, J. H.—*Primer for Protestants*
Smith, P.—*The Age of the Reformation*
Smith, P.—*Erasmus*
Stone, J. M.—*Reformation and Renaissance*
Vedder, H. C.—*The Reformation in Germany*
Walker, W.—*John Calvin*
Wace, H.—*Principles of the Reformation*
Wenger, J. C.—*Glimpses of Mennonite History and Doctrine*

PART IV: THE MODERN CHURCH

AMERICAN CHURCH HISTORY SERIES
Baron, S. W.—*Modern Nationalism and Religion*
Bates, S. M.—*Religious Liberty*
Brown, C.—*The Larger Faith*
Brown, W. A.—*Imperialistic Religion and the Religion of Democracy*
Brown, W. A.—*The New Order in the Church*
Burkhart, R. A.—*How the Church Grows*
Cooke, G. W.—*Unitarianism in America*
Dexter, H. M.—*A Handbook of Congregationalism*
Fosdick, H. E.—*The Modern Use of the Bible*
INTERSEMINARY SERIES
Jones, R. M.—*The Quakers in the American Colonies*
Leiper, H. S.—*Christianity Today*
McGlothlin, W. J.—*The Course of Christian History*
MADRAS SERIES (7 volumes)
Mott, J. R.—Addresses and Papers
Neve, J. L.—*Brief History of the Lutheran Church in America*
Oldham, J. H.—*The Oxford Conference*
Rowe, H.—*History of Religions in the United States*
Schaff, P.—*Creeds of Christendom*
Soares, T. G.—*A Baptist Manual*
Sweet, W. W.—*Religion on the American Frontier*
Van Dusen, H. P.—*World Christianity*
Van Kirk, W. W.—*A Christian Global Strategy*
Year Book of American Churches

INDEX